Crochet with Style

Crochet with Style

Fun-to-Make
Sweaters for All Seasons

Melissa Leapman

The Taunton Press

Publisher: JIM CHILDS

Acquisitions Editor: JOLYNN GOWER

Assistant Editor: SARAH COE

Editor: CANDACE B. LEVY

Technical Editor: ANN E. SMITH

Cover Designer: AMY YOUNG

Interior Designers: AMY YOUNG AND ROSALIND WANKE

Layout Artist: ROSALIE VACCARO

Photographer: JACK DEUTSCH

Illustrators: MELISSA LEAPMAN AND MARIO FERRO

Taunton
BOOKS & VIDEOS

for fellow enthusiasts

Printed in the United States of America

10 9 8 7 6 5 4 3 2 1

The Taunton Press, Inc., 63 South Main Street, PO Box 5506,
Newtown, CT 06470-5506
e-mail: tp@taunton.com

Distributed by Publishers Group West

Library of Congress Cataloging-in-Publication Data
Leapman, Melissa.
  Crochet with style : fun-to-make sweaters for all seasons / Melissa Leapman.
    p.   cm.
  ISBN 1-56158-339-1
    1. Crocheting—Patterns. 2. Sweaters. I. Title.
TT825.L388   2000
746.43'40432—dc21   00-030267

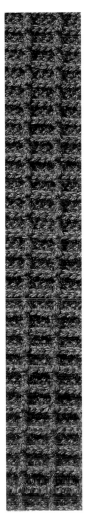

For my brother, Mark, the recipient of the very first crocheted garment I ever made, with love.

Acknowledgments

I wish to thank the following crocheters who worked hard to create the beautiful sample sweaters in this book: Ceal Ebert, Marianne Forrestal, Carole Minchew, JoAnn Moss, Sharon Ryman, and Pat Yankee. Their expertise and enthusiasm helped make the designing and pattern-writing process easier and more fun for me.

Thanks are due, too, to the many yarn and button companies who generously provided materials for the sweaters.

Special thanks go to Kathleen Power Johnson and Melinda Thomsen for their years of friendship and encouragement, and to Ann E. Smith for painstakingly editing the patterns.

For many years of love and encouragement, I am most grateful to Michael Blowney.

Contents

Introduction

If you are like me, you just love the way it feels to wear a new sweater you created—especially when everyone compliments you on both your appearance and your skill!

For this book, I have created a collection of 24 great-looking crocheted garments. A variety of techniques, yarns, and skill levels are included in these projects, from the traditional Motif-Bordered Tunic to the more contemporary Interlocked Triangles Jacket.

They all are, I hope, as much fun to make as they will be to wear!

Happy Crocheting!

Shaded Shells Pullover

Waves of color grace this elegant shell-stitch design. The easy scalloped trim that accents the borders is the perfect finishing touch.

INTERMEDIATE

❀ *Sizes*

Small (Medium, Large, Extra-Large). Instructions are for smallest size, with changes for other sizes noted in parentheses as necessary.

❀ *Finished Measurements*

Bust: 38 (42, 46, 50)"/96.5 (106.5, 116.5, 127) cm
Length: 27½ (28½, 28½, 29½)"/70 (72.5, 72.5, 75) cm
Sleeve width at upper arm: 18 (18, 20, 20)"/45.5 (45.5, 51, 51) cm

❀ *Materials*

Bernat's *Country Garden* DK (light worsted weight; 100% wool; 1¾ oz/50 g; approx 135 yd/124 m), 4 (4, 5, 6) balls Juniper #56 (A), 6 (7, 8, 9) balls *each* of Whaler Blue #35 (B) and Mist Blue #34 (C), and 3 (4, 5, 6) balls Snowdrop #01 (D)
Crochet hook, size F/5 (3.75 mm) or size needed to obtain gauge

❀ *Gauge*

In patt, measured across the widest point, four 5-dc dec = 4"/10 cm wide.
To measure your gauge, make a test swatch as follows: With A, ch 28. Work Shaded Shell Patt for 10 rows. Fasten off.
Piece should measure 4½"/11.5 cm wide and 3½"/9 cm long. **To save time, take time to check gauge.**

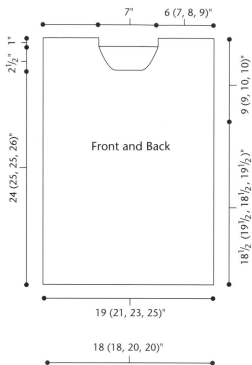

7" 6 (7, 8, 9)"

2½" 1"

9 (9, 10, 10)"

Front and Back

24 (25, 25, 26)"

18½ (19½, 18½, 19½)"

19 (21, 23, 25)"

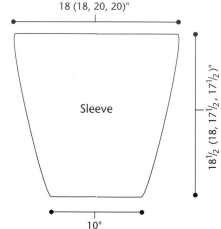

18 (18, 20, 20)"

Sleeve

18½ (18, 17½, 17½)"

10"

❋ PATTERN NOTES:

- 5-dc dec = Holding back last loop, work dc into next 5 sts, yarn over and draw it through all 6 loops on hook.
- 3-dc dec = Holding back last loop, work dc into next 3 sts, yarn over and draw it through all 4 loops on hook.
- To change color, work until 2 loops rem on hook; with second color, complete the st; fasten off first color.
- For a description and illustration of any unfamiliar stitch, refer to the back of the book.

❋ Shaded Shells Patt

Ch multiple of 6 + 4

Foundation Row (RS): 2 dc into fourth ch from hook, *skip next 2 ch, sc into next ch, skip next 2 ch, 5 dc into next ch (*shell made*). Repeat from * across, ending row with skip next 2 ch, sc into next ch, skip next 2 ch, 3 dc into last ch. Change color, ch 1, turn.

Row 1 (WS): Sc into first dc, *ch 3, 5-dc dec to combine the next 5 sts, ch 3, sc into next dc. Repeat from * across, ending row with ch 3, 5-dc dec to combine the next 5 sts, ch 3, sc into top of turning-ch-3. Ch 3, turn.

Row 2: 2 dc into first sc, *sc into next 5-dc dec, 5 dc into next sc. Repeat from * across, ending row with sc into next 5-dc dec, 3 dc into last sc. Change color, ch 1, turn.

Repeat Rows 1 and 2 in Color Sequence for patt.

❋ Color Sequence

1 row A
*2 rows B
2 rows C
2 rows D
2 rows C
2 rows B
2 rows A

Repeat from * for patt.

❋ Back

With A, ch 118 (130, 142, 154). Work Foundation Row of Shaded Shell Patt—18 (20, 22, 24) 5-dc shells across.

Cont even in patt until piece measures approx 26½ (27½, 27½, 28½)"/67.5 (70, 70, 72.5) cm from beg, ending after WS row.

Shape Neck: Next Row (RS): Ch 3, turn, 2 dc into first sc, (sc into next 5-dc dec, 5 dc into next sc) 5 (6, 7, 8) times, sc into next 5-dc dec, 3 dc into next sc. Ch 1, turn, leaving rest of row unworked.

Next Row (Straight Edge Row) (WS): Sc into first st, *hdc into next st, dc into next 3 sts, hdc into next st, sc into next st. Repeat from * across to end row. Fasten off.

For second side of neck, with RS facing, skip the middle seven 5-dc dec sts and attach yarn with a slip st to next sc and ch 3. Complete as for first side.

❊ Front

Work as for back until piece measures approx 24 (25, 25, 26)"/61 (63.5, 63.5, 66) cm from beg, ending after WS row.

Shape Neck: Next Row (RS): Ch 3, turn, 2 dc into first sc, (sc into next 5-dc dec, 5 dc into next sc) 7 (8, 9, 10) times, sc into next 5-dc dec. Fasten off. Turn.

Next Row: With WS facing, skip last 3 sts made on last row and attach yarn with a slip st to next st and ch 1. Sc into next st, cont in patt as established to end row. Ch 3, turn.

Next Row: 2 dc into first sc, (sc into next 5-dc dec, 5 dc into next sc) 6 (7, 8, 9) times, sc into next 5-dc dec. Fasten off.

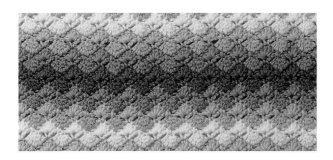

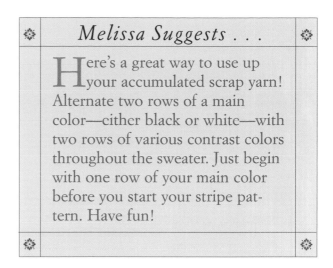

Next Row: With WS facing, skip the last 3 sts made on last row and attach yarn with a slip st to next st and ch 1. Sc into next st, cont in patt as established to end row.

Cont even until piece measures same as back, working last row same as Straight Edge Row on back. Fasten off.

For second side of neck, with RS facing, skip the middle three 5-dc dec sts and attach yarn with a slip st to next 5-dc dec and ch 1.

Next Row (RS): Sc into same 5-dc dec as slip st, 5 dc into next sc, cont in patt as established to end row. Ch 1, turn.

Next Row: Sc into first dc, (ch 3, 5 dc dec, ch 3, sc into next dc) 7 (8, 9, 10) times. *Do not ch 3 to turn.*

Next Row: Slip st to top of first 5-dc dec, ch 1, sc into same place as last slip st, (5 dc into next sc, sc into next 5-dc dec) 6 (7, 8, 9) times, 3 dc into last sc in row. Change color, ch 1, turn.

Next Row: Sc into first dc, (ch 3, 5-dc dec, ch 3, sc into next dc) 6 (7, 8, 9) times. Ch 1, turn.

Complete as for first side.

❀ Sleeves

With A, ch 64. Work Foundation Row of Shaded Shells Patt—six 5-dc shells across.

Work Row 1 of Shaded Shells Patt, ch 3, turn.

Next Row: 4 dc into first sc, *sc into next 5-dc dec, 5 dc into next sc. Repeat from * across, ending row with sc into next 5-dc dec, 5 dc into last sc. Change color, ch 3, turn.

Next Row: Skip first dc, dc into next dc, *ch 3, sc into next dc, ch 3, 5-dc dec to combine next 5 sts. Repeat from * across, ending row with ch 3, sc into next dc, ch 3, dec dc. Ch 1, turn.

Next Row: Sc into dec dc, *5 dc into next sc, sc into next 5-dc dec. Repeat from * across, ending row with 5 dc into next sc, sc into top of turning-ch-3. Change color, ch 3, turn.

Next Row: Skip first dc, dec dc, *ch 3, sc into next dc, ch 3, 5-dc dec. Repeat from * across, ending row with ch 3, sc into next dc, ch 3, 3-dc dec. Ch 3, turn.

Next Row: 2 dc into 3-dc dec, sc into same 3-dc dec, *5 dc into next sc, sc into next 5-dc dec. Repeat from * across, ending row with 5 dc into next sc, (sc, 3 dc) into top of turning-ch-3. Change color, ch 1, turn.

Next 7 (7, 5, 5) rows: Work even in patt as established.

Repeat last 12 (12, 10, 10) rows 2 (2, 3, 3) more times, then work first five rows once.

Work even until sleeve measures approx 18½ (18, 17½, 17½)"/47 (45.5, 44.5, 44.5) cm from beg, working last row same as Straight Edge Row on back. Fasten off.

❀ Finishing

Sew shoulder seams.

Neckband: With RS facing, join A with a slip st at neck edge of right shoulder seam and ch 1.

Rnd 1: Work 90 sc evenly around neckline. Join with a slip st to first sc. Ch 1.

Rnd 2: Sc into same sc as last slip st, *skip next 2 sc, 5 dc into next sc, skip next 2 sc, sc into next sc. Repeat from * around, ending rnd with skip next 2 sc, 5 dc into next sc, skip next 2 sc, slip st to first sc. Fasten off.

Place markers 9 (9, 10, 10)"/23 (23, 25.5, 25.5) cm down from shoulders.

Set in sleeves between markers. Sew sleeve and side seams.

Bottom Border: With RS facing, attach A with a slip st to lower right side seam and ch 1.

Rnd 1: Working into unworked loops of foundation ch, work 228 (252, 276, 300) sc around lower edge. Join with slip st to first sc. Ch 1.

Rnd 2: Sc into same sc as last slip st, *skip next 2 sc, 5 dc into next sc, skip next 2 sc, sc into next sc. Repeat from * around, ending rnd with skip next 2 sc, 5 dc into next sc, skip next 2 sc, slip st to first sc. Fasten off.

Sleeve Border: With RS facing, attach A with a slip st to lower sleeve seam and ch 1.

Rnd 1: Working into unused loops of foundation ch, work 60 sc around lower edge. Join with a slip st to first sc. Ch 1.

Rnd 2: Sc into same sc as last slip st, *skip next 2 sc, 5 dc into next sc, skip next 2 sc, sc into next sc. Repeat from * around, ending rnd with skip next 2 sc, 5 dc into next sc, skip next 2 sc, slip st to first sc. Fasten off.

Motif-Bordered Tunic

Here's a new twist on every crocheter's favorite. A simple V-stitch pattern evolves into an elegant sweater when bordered by these updated motifs.

❖ *Sizes*

Small/Medium (Large/Extra-Large). Instructions are for smaller size, with changes for the larger size noted in parentheses as necessary.

❖ *Finished Measurements*

Bust: 42 (54)"/106.5 (137) cm
Length (Including Edging): 30 (31)"/76 (79) cm
Sleeve width at upper arm: 15 (17)"/38 (43) cm

❖ *Materials*

Classic Elite's *Provence* (light worsted weight; 100% cotton; 4 oz/125 g; approx
    256 yd/233 m), 7 (9) hanks White #2601
Crochet hooks, sizes E/4 and F/5 (3.50 and 3.75 mm) or size needed to obtain
    gauge
Yarn needle

❖ *Gauge*

With smaller hook, each motif measures 3"/7.5 cm square.
With larger hook, 9 V-Sts and 10 rows measure 5"/12.5 cm.
To measure your gauge in V-St Patt, make a test swatch as follows: Ch 27 with
    larger hook. Sc into 2nd ch from hook and into each ch across—26 sc. Ch 3,
    turn. Work V-St Patt on 8 V-Sts plus 1 dc each side for eight rows. Fasten off.
Piece should measure 4¾"/12 cm wide and 4"/10 cm long. **To save time, take time
    to check gauge.**

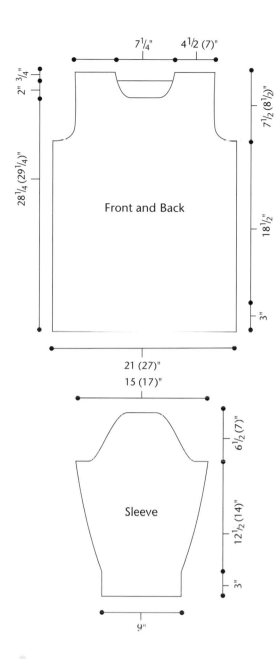

Front and Back

7¹/₄"   4¹/₂ (7)"

2" ³/₄"

28¹/₄ (29¹/₄)"

7¹/₂ (8¹/₂)"

18¹/₂"

3"

21 (27)"

15 (17)"

Sleeve

6¹/₂ (7)"

12¹/₂ (14)"

3"

9"

Pattern Notes:

- V-St = (Dc, ch 1, dc) into indicated st.
- Dec dc-tr = Yarn over, insert hook into first dc of next V-St and pull up a loop, yarn over and draw it through 2 loops on hook, yarn over twice and insert hook into top of turning-ch and pull up a loop, (yarn over and draw it through 2 loops on hook) twice, yarn over and draw it through all 3 loops on hook.
- Each turning-ch-3 counts as a dc.
- Each ch-1 sp counts as a st.
- For a description and illustration of any unfamiliar stitch, refer to the back of the book.

❊ Motif

Ch 5. Join with a slip st to form a ring. Ch 1.

Rnd 1: Work 8 sc into ring. Join with a slip st to first sc. Ch 1.

Rnd 2: Sc into same sc as slip st, *ch 5, sc into next sc, ch 8, sc into next sc. Repeat from * around, ending rnd with ch 5, sc into next sc, ch 8, slip st into first sc, slip st into next ch-5 sp. Ch 1.

Rnd 3: Sc into same ch-5 sp as slip st, *ch 5, sc into next ch-sp. Repeat from * around, ending rnd with ch 5, slip st into top of first sc, slip st into next ch-sp.

Rnd 4: Ch 3, 2 dc into same ch-sp as slip st, *(3 dc, ch 3, 3 dc) into next sc, 3 dc into next ch-5 sp, skip next sc, 3 dc into next ch-5 sp. Repeat from * around, ending rnd with (3 dc, ch 3, 3 dc) into next sc, 3 dc into next ch-5 sp, skip next sc, slip st into top of ch-3. Fasten off.

❊ V-St Patt

Foundation Row (RS): Skip first 2 sc, *V-St into next sc, skip next 2 sc. Repeat from * across, ending row with V-St into next sc, skip next sc, dc into last sc. Ch 3, turn.

Patt Row: Skip first dc, *V-St into next ch-1 sp. Repeat from * across, ending row with dc into top of turning-ch-3. Ch 3, turn.

Repeat Patt Row.

❊ Back

With smaller hook, make 7 (9) motifs. Whipstitch them tog *through the back loops* into a strip.

With RS facing and larger hook, attach yarn with a slip st to upper-right corner and ch 1. Work 107 (137) sc evenly along top edge of strip. Ch 1, turn.

Next Row: Sc into each sc across. Ch 3, turn.

Beg V-St Patt, and work even on 35 (45) V-Sts plus 1 dc each side until piece measures approx 21½"/54.5 cm from beg, ending after WS row. *Do not ch 3 to turn.*

Shape Armholes: Next Row (RS): Slip st into first 7 sts, ch 3, *V-St into next ch-1 sp. Repeat from * across until 2 V-Sts plus 1 dc rem in row, ending row with dc into first dc of next V-St. Ch 4, turn.

Next Row: Skip first 2 dc and ch-1 sp, dc into next dc, *V-St into next ch-1 sp. Repeat from * across until 1 V-St plus 1 dc rem in row, ending row with dec dc-tr to combine the first dc of the next V-St and the turning-ch. Ch 4, turn.

Repeat last row 2 (4) more times—25 (31) V-Sts plus 1 dc each side rem.

Cont even until piece measures approx 28¼ (29¼)"/72 (74.5) cm from beg, ending after WS row. Ch 3, turn.

Shape Neck: Next Row (RS): Skip first dc, *V-St into next ch-1 sp. Repeat from * 5 (8) more times, dc into first dc of next V-st. Ch 3, turn.

Work even for one more row. Fasten off.

For second side of neck, with RS facing, skip the middle 13 ch-sps, join yarn with a slip st to next dc to the left of last ch-1 sp and complete as for first side.

❀ Front

Work as for back until piece measures approx 26¼ (27¼)"/66.5 (69) cm, ending after WS row. Ch 3, turn.

Shape Neck: Neck Shaping Row 1 (RS): Skip first dc, *V-St into next ch-1 sp. Repeat from * 7 (10) more times, ending row with dc into top of first dc of next V-St. Ch 4, turn.

Neck Shaping Row 2: Skip first 2 dc and ch-1 sp, dc into next dc, *V-St into next ch-1 sp. Repeat from * across, ending row with dc into top of turning-ch-3. Ch 3, turn.

Neck Shaping Row 3: Skip first dc, *V-St into next ch-1 sp. Repeat from * across, ending row with dec dc-tr to combine first dc of last V-St and turning-ch. Ch 3, turn.

Cont even until piece measures same as back to shoulder. Fasten off.

For second side of neck, with RS facing, skip the middle 9 ch-1 sps and join yarn with a slip st to next dc. Work in patt to end row. Ch 3, turn.

Next Row (WS): Work same as Neck Shaping Row 3. Ch 3, turn.

Next Row: Work same as Neck Shaping Row 2.

Complete as for first side.

❀ Sleeves

With smaller hook, make 3 motifs. Whipstitch them tog *through the back loops* into a strip.

With RS facing and larger hook, attach yarn with a slip st to upper-right corner and ch 1. Work 47 sc evenly along top edge of strip. Ch 1, turn.

Next Row (WS): Sc into each sc across. Ch 3, turn.

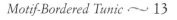

Work one row of V-St Patt—15 V-Sts plus 1 dc each side. Ch 4, turn.

Inc Row 1: Dc into first dc, *V-St into next ch-1 sp. Repeat from * across, ending row with V-St into top of turning-ch. Ch 4, turn.

Inc Row 2: Dc into first ch-1 sp, *V-St into next ch-1 sp. Repeat from * across, ending row with V-St into top of turning-ch. Ch 3, turn.

Inc Row 3: V-St into first ch-1 sp, *V-St into next ch-1 sp. Repeat from * across, ending row with V-St in turning-ch, dc into third ch of turning-ch. Ch 3, turn.

Inc Row 4: Skip first dc, *V-St into next ch-1 sp. Repeat from * across, ending row with dc into top of turning-ch-3. Ch 4, turn.

Repeat Inc Rows 1–4 a total of 5 (6) more times—27 (29) V-Sts plus 1 dc each side.

Work even by repeating Inc Row 4 until sleeve measures approx 15½ (17)"/39.5 (43) cm from beg, ending after WS row. *Do not ch to turn.*

Shape Cap. Next Row (RS): Slip st into first 2 dc and ch 1 sp, slip st into next 2 dc and ch-1 sp, slip st into next dc, ch 3, *V-St into next ch-1 sp. Repeat from * across until 2 V-Sts plus 1 dc rem in row, ending row with dc into first dc of next V-St. Ch 3, turn.

Dec Row 1: Skip first 2 dc and ch-1 sp, dc into next dc, *V-St into next ch-1 sp. Repeat from * across until one V-St plus 1 dc rem in row, ending row with dec dc-tr to combine the first dc of next V-St and turning-ch. Ch 3, turn.

Dec Row 2: Skip first dec dc-tr, V-St into next ch-1 sp. Repeat from * across, ending row with dc into top of turning-ch. Ch 3, turn.

Repeat Dec Row 1 for 9 (10) more times—3 V-Sts plus 1 dc each side rem.

Work 1 row even. Fasten off.

❧ Finishing

Lower Front Edging: With RS facing and smaller hook, attach yarn to corner ch-3 sp of first motif and ch 1.

Row 1 (RS): Work 102 (132) sc along edge. Ch 1, turn.

Row 2: Sc into each sc across. Ch 1, turn.

Row 3: Sc into first 3 sc, *ch 3, slip st into third ch from hook, sc into next 3 sc. Repeat from * across. Fasten off.

Lower Back Edging: Work as for the Lower Front Edging.

Lower Sleeve Edging: With RS facing and smaller hook, attach yarn to lower right corner of first motif and ch 1.

Row 1 (RS): Work 42 sc along edge.

Complete as for Lower Front and Back Edgings.

Sew shoulder seams.

Neckband: With RS facing and smaller hook, attach yarn with a slip st to neck edge of right shoulder seam and ch 1.

Rnd 1 (RS): Work 84 sc around neckline, working a dec sc each side at beg of back neck shaping. Join with slip st to first sc.

Rnd 2: Ch 1, *sc into next 3 sc, ch 3, slip st into third ch from hook. Repeat from * around, ending rnd with slip st to first sc. Fasten off.

Set in sleeves. Sew sleeve and side seams.

Oversized Nubby Cardigan

Cuddle up in this richly textured cardigan. The style is reminiscent of your boyfriend's sweater, but this one actually fits!

INTERMEDIATE

❈ *Sizes*

Small (Medium, Large, Extra-Large). Instructions are for smallest size, with changes for other sizes noted in parentheses as necessary.

❈ *Finished Measurements*

Bust (Buttoned): 38½ (43, 47¼, 52)"/98 (109, 120, 132) cm
Length: 26 (27, 28, 29)"/66 (68.5, 71, 73.5) cm
Sleeve width at upper arm: 18 (19, 19¾, 21)"/45.5 (48.5, 50, 53.5) cm

❈ *Materials*

Patons's *Decor* (worsted weight; 75% Acrilan® acrylic/25% wool; 3½ oz/100 g; approx 210 yd/192 m), 7 (8, 9, 9) skeins Rich Grey Heather #1673 (A), 3 (4, 4, 5) skeins each of Grey Heather #1672 (B) and Aran #1602 (C)
Crochet hooks, sizes G/6 and H/8 (4.25 and 5.00 mm) or size needed to obtain gauge
Six ¾"/19 mm buttons (JHB International's *Serpentine Style* #96453 was used on sample garment)

❈ *Gauge*

In patt with larger hook, 14 sts and 10 rows = 4"/10 cm.
To measure your gauge, make a test swatch as follows: With larger hook, ch 23. Work Nubby Patt on 21 sts for 10 rows. Fasten off.
Piece should measure 6"/15 cm wide and 4"/10 cm long. **To save time, take time to check gauge.**

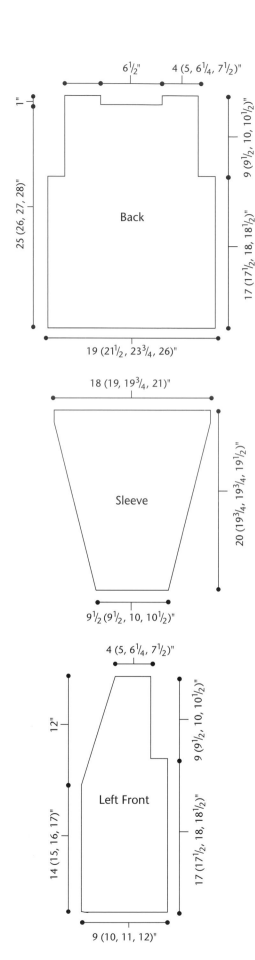

Back

6½" 4 (5, 6¼, 7½)"

1"

9 (9½, 10, 10½)"

25 (26, 27, 28)"

17 (17½, 18, 18½)"

19 (21½, 23¾, 26)"

Sleeve

18 (19, 19¾, 21)"

20 (19¾, 19¾, 19½)"

9½ (9½, 10, 10½)"

Left Front

4 (5, 6¼, 7½)"

12"

9 (9½, 10, 10½)"

14 (15, 16, 17)"

17 (17½, 18, 18½)"

9 (10, 11, 12)"

Pattern Notes:

- Each turning-ch-3 counts as 1 dc.
- To decrease in dc, work until 2 sts rem in row, then work a dec dc to combine the last 2 sts in row. On the next row, work last st into the last dc, not into the top of the turning-ch-3.
- To decrease in sc, work a dec sc to combine the first 2 sts and the last 2 sts of the row.
- To increase, work 2 sts into a st.
- To change color, work until 2 loops rem on hook; with second color, complete the st; fasten off first color.
- For a description and illustration of any unfamiliar stitch, refer to the back of the book.

❀ Nubby Patt

Ch multiple of 2 + 1

Foundation Row (RS): Dc into fourth ch from hook and into each ch across. Change color, ch 1, turn.

Row 1 (WS): Sc into first dc, *tr into next dc, sc into next sc. Repeat from * across, ending row with tr into next dc, sc into top of turning-ch-3. Change color, ch 3, turn.

Row 2: Skip first sc, dc into each st across. Change color, ch 1, turn.

Repeat Rows 1 and 2 in Color Sequence for patt.

❀ Stripe Patt

1 row A

1 row B

1 row A

1 row C

Repeat for patt.

❀ Back

With larger hook and A, ch 69 (77, 85, 93). Beg Nubby Patt in Stripe Patt, and work even on 67 (75, 83, 91) sts until piece measures approx 17 (17½, 18, 18½)"/43 (44.5, 45.5, 47) cm from beg, ending after RS row. Fasten off A.

Shape Armholes: Next Row (WS): Skip first 8 sts, attach next color with a slip st to next st and ch 1. Sc into same dc as slip st, *tr into next dc, sc into next dc. Repeat from * across until 8 sts rem. Change color, ch 3, turn, leaving rest of row unworked—51 (59, 67, 75) sts.

Cont even in patt until piece measures approx 25 (26, 27, 28)"/63.5 (66, 68.5, 71) cm from beg, ending after WS row.

Shape Neck: Next Row (RS): Work across first 14 (18, 22, 26) sts, turn.

Cont even on these shoulder sts until piece measures approx 26 (27, 28, 29)"/66 (68.5, 71, 73.5) cm from beg. Fasten off.

For second side of neck, with RS facing, skip the middle 23 sts, join yarn with a slip st to next st, ch 3, and complete as for first side.

❀ Pocket Lining (Make Two)

With larger hook and A, ch 20.

Foundation Row: Sc into second ch from hook and into each ch across—19 sc. Ch 1, turn.

Next Row: Sc into each sc across. Ch 1, turn.

Repeat last row until lining measures approx 5½"/14 cm from beg. Fasten off.

❀ Left Front

With larger hook and A, ch 33 (37, 41, 45). Beg Nubby Patt in Stripe Patt, and work even on 31 (35, 39, 43) sts until piece measures approx 6½"/16.5 cm from beg, ending after WS row.

Place Pocket Lining: Next Row (RS): Cont in patt and work across first 6 (8, 10, 12) sts, with RS facing cont in patt across 19 sts of one pocket lining, skip next 19 sts of main fabric on left front, work rem sts on front to end row.

Cont even until piece measures approx 14 (15, 16, 17)"/35.5 (38, 40.5, 43) cm from beg, ending after RS row. Change color, ch 1, turn.

Shape Neck: Next Row (RS): Dec 1 st at beg of next row and then every other row four more times, then every fourth row four times; **and at the same time,** when piece measures approx 17 (17½, 18, 18½)"/43 (44.5, 45.5, 47) cm from beg, end after WS row and **Shape Armhole** as follows: Skip first 8 sts and attach A with a slip st to next st and ch 3. Cont across row in patt as established.

After all neck decreases have been completed, work even until piece measures same as back to shoulders. Fasten off.

❖ Right Front

Work as for left front until piece measures approx 14 (15, 16, 17)"/35.5 (38, 40.5, 43) cm from beg, ending after WS row. Change color, ch 3, turn.

Shape Neck: Next Row (RS): Dec 1 st at beg of next row and then every other row four more times, then every fourth row four times; **and at the same time,** when piece measures approx 17 (17½, 18, 18½)"/43 (44.5, 45.5, 47) cm from beg, end after WS row and **Shape Armhole** as follows.

Next Row (RS): Work across row in patt as established until 8 sts rem in row. Turn, leaving last 8 sts of row unworked.

Complete as for left front.

❖ Sleeves

With larger hook and A, ch 35 (35, 37, 39). Beg Nubby Patt in Stripe Patt on 33 (33, 35, 37) sts for two rows. Change color, ch 3, turn.

Inc 1 st each side every other row 10 (15, 16, 17) times, then every fourth row 5 (2, 1, 1) times—63 (67, 69, 73) sts.

Cont even until sleeve measures approx 20 (19¾, 19¾, 19½)"/51 (50, 50, 49.5) cm from beg, ending after RS row. Fasten off.

❖ Finishing

Sew shoulder seams.

Pocket Edgings: With RS facing and smaller hook, attach A with a slip st to top of pocket opening

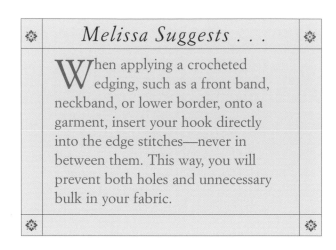

and ch 1. Work 2 rows sc along top of pocket. Fasten off.

Sew sides of pocket edge to front. Sew pocket linings to WS of front.

Front Bands: With RS facing and smaller hook, attach A with a slip st to right front edge and ch 1. Work sc evenly along right front, across back of neck and down left front. Ch 1, turn.

Cont in sc, working 2 sc at each side at beg of front neck shaping and dec sc each side of back neck shaping, until band measures approx ¾"/2 cm from beg. Place markers for six evenly spaced buttonholes along right front, making the first ¼"/ 0.5 cm from beg of neck shaping and the last ½"/1.5 cm from bottom edge.

Next Row: Cont in sc as before, and make six buttonholes by working (ch 2, skip next 2 sc) where marked.

On next row, work 2 sc into each ch-2 sp of previous row.

Cont in sc as before until band measures approx 1½"/4 cm. Fasten off.

Set in sleeves. Sew sleeve and side seams.

Place markers for 6 evenly spaced buttons along left front edge, making them opposite ch-2 buttonhole spaces. Sew on buttons.

Nautical V-Neck Pullover

Dive into this project, with its interesting striping technique that gives maximum effect with minimum effort.

INTERMEDIATE

❖ *Sizes*

Small (Medium, Large, Extra-Large). Instructions are for smallest size, with changes for other sizes noted in parentheses as necessary.

❖ *Finished Measurements*

Bust: 39½ (43, 46, 49)"/100.5 (109, 117, 124.5) cm
Length: 24¾ (26, 27½, 27½)"/63 (66, 70, 70) cm
Sleeve width at upper arm: 14½ (15, 15½, 15½)"/36.5
   (38, 39.5, 39.5) cm

❖ *Materials*

Paton's *Cotton DK* (light worsted weight; 100% cotton; 1¾ oz/50 g; approx
  116 yd/106 m), 14 (15, 16, 17) balls Ship Blue #6311 (A) and 6 (7, 8, 8) balls
  Snowball White #6301 (B)
Crochet hooks, sizes E/4 and F/5 (3.50 and 3.75 mm) or size needed to obtain
  gauge

❖ *Gauge*

In patt with larger hook, 20 sts and 16 rows = 4"/10 cm.
To measure your gauge, make a test swatch as follows: Ch 25 with larger hook.
  Work Textured Patt on 23 sts for 16 rows. Fasten off.
Piece should measure 4½"/11.5 cm wide and 4"/10 cm long. **To save time, take
time to check gauge.**

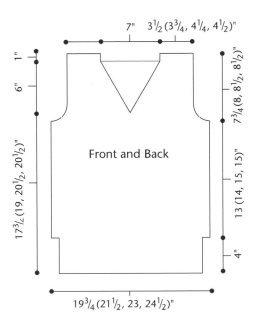

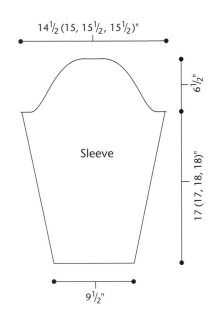

Pattern Notes:

- Triple dec sc = (Insert hook into next st and draw up a loop) three times, yarn over and draw it through all 4 loops on hook.
- Each turning-ch-3 counts as a dc.
- To decrease in dc, work until 2 sts rem in row, then work a dec dc to combine the last 2 sts in row. On the next row, work last st into the last dc, not into the top of the turning-ch-3.
- To decrease in sc, work a dec sc to combine the first 2 sts and the last 2 sts of the row.
- To increase, work 2 sts into a st.
- To change color, work until 2 loops rem on hook; with second color, complete the st; fasten off first color.
- For a description and illustration of any unfamiliar stitch, refer to the back of the book.

❖ Textured Patt

With A, ch multiple of 8 + 1

Foundation Row (WS): Dc into fourth ch from hook and into each ch across. Ch 1, turn.

Row 1 (RS): Sc into each dc across, ending row with sc into third ch of turning-ch-3. Ch 1, turn.

Row 2: Sc into each sc across. Change to B, ch 1, turn.

Row 3: Sc into first 7 sc, *ch 4, sc into st at base of next dc three rows below, ch 4, skip next sc from last row, sc into next 7 sc. Repeat from * across, change to A, ch 3, turn.

Row 4: Skip first sc, dc into next 6 sc, *dc into skipped sc two rows below, dc into next 7 sc. Repeat from * across. Ch 1, turn.

Rows 5 and 6: Work same as Rows 1 and 2. At the end of Row 6, change to B, ch 1, turn.

Row 7: Sc into first 3 sc, *ch 4, sc into st at base of next dc three rows below, ch 4, skip next sc from last row, sc into next 7 sc. Repeat from * across, ending row with ch 4, sc into st at base of next dc three rows below, ch 4, skip next sc from last row, sc into last 3 sc. Change to A, ch 3, turn.

Row 8: Skip first sc, dc into next 2 sc, *dc into skipped sc two rows below, dc into next 7 sc. Repeat from * across, ending row with dc into skipped sc two rows below, dc into last 3 sc. Ch 1, turn.

Repeat Rows 1–8 for patt.

❀ Back

With larger hook and A, ch 97 (105, 113, 121). Work Textured Patt on 95 (103, 111, 119) sts until piece measures approx 4"/10 cm from beg, ending after Row 7 of patt.

Side Slit Closure: Next Row (WS): With A, ch 5 to turn instead of ch 3. Dc into fourth ch from hook and into next ch, dc into next 3 sc, *dc into skipped sc two rows below, dc into next 7 sc. Repeat from * across, ending row with dc into skipped sc two rows below, dc into last 3 sc. Ch 3, turn.

Next Row (RS): Sc into second ch from hook and into next ch, cont in patt to end row—99 (107, 115, 123) sc total.

Cont even until piece measures approx 17 (18, 19, 19)"/43 (45.5, 48.5, 48.5) cm from beg, ending after Row 3 or 7 of Textured Patt.

Shape Armholes: Next Row (WS): Change to A, ch 1, slip st into first 7 sts, ch 3, work in patt as established across row until 6 sts rem—87 (95, 103, 111) sts total—leave last 6 sts unworked, ch 1, turn.

Next Row: Slip st into first 2 sts, ch 1, work in patt as established across row until 2 sts rem—83 (91, 99, 107) sts total—leave last 2 sts unworked, ch 1, turn.

Repeat last row 1 (2, 3, 3) more times—79 (83, 87, 95) sts total.

Cont patt as established and dec 1 st each side every other row 4 (5, 5, 7) times—71 (73, 77, 81) sts rem.

Cont even until piece measures approx 23¾ (25, 26½, 26½)"/60.5 (63.5, 67.5, 67.5) cm from beg, ending after WS row.

Shape Neck: Next Row (RS): Work across first 18 (19, 21, 23) sts, turn.

Cont even on these shoulder sts until piece measures approx 24¾ (26, 27½, 27½)"/63 (66, 70, 70) cm from beg. Fasten off.

For second side of neck, with RS facing, skip the middle 35 sts, join yarn with a slip st to next st and complete as for first side.

❀ Front

Work same as back until piece measures approx 17¾ (19, 20½, 20½)"/45 (48.5, 52, 52) cm from beg, ending after WS row.

Mark center st with a safety pin. Cont armhole shaping same as back and, **at the same time, Shape Neck** as follows.

Next Row (RS): Work across until and including 1 st before the marked center st, ch 1, turn.

Working on left shoulder only, dec 1 st at neck edge every row eleven more times, then every other row five times.

Work even on rem 18 (19, 21, 23) sts until piece measures same as back to shoulder. Fasten off.

For right shoulder, with RS facing, skip the middle st, join yarn with a slip st to next st and complete as for left shoulder.

❀ Sleeves

With larger hook and A, ch 49.

Work Textured Patt on 47 sts until sleeve measures 2"/5 cm from beg.

Next Row: Inc 1 st each side—49 sts.

Color-Block Pullover

Here's a design to flatter every figure. The basic seed stitch pattern makes it a cinch to crochet!

❀ Sizes

X-Small (Small, Medium, Large, X-Large). Instructions are for smallest size, with changes for other sizes noted in parentheses as necessary.

❀ Finished Measurements

Bust: 36½ (41, 45, 49, 53)"/92.5 (104, 114.5, 124.5, 134.5) cm
Length: 27 (27, 28½, 28½, 28½)"/68.5 (68.5, 72.5, 72.5, 72.5) cm
Sleeve width at upper arm: 15 (15, 15¾, 15¾, 15¾)"/38
   (38, 40, 40, 40) cm

❀ Materials

Paton's *Decor* (worsted weight; 75% Acrilan® acrylic/25% wool; 3½ oz/100 g; approx 210 yd/192 m), 4 (4, 5, 6, 6) skeins *each* of Navy #1643 (A), Rich Periwinkle #1642 (B), and Periwinkle #1641 (C)
Crochet hooks, sizes G/6 and H/8 (4.25 and 5.00 mm) or size needed to obtain gauge

❀ Gauge

In patt with larger hook, 19 sts and 16 rows = 4"/10 cm.
To measure your gauge, make a test swatch as follows: Ch 20. Work Seed St Patt for 16 rows. Fasten off.
Piece should measure 4"/10 cm square. **To save time, take time to check gauge.**

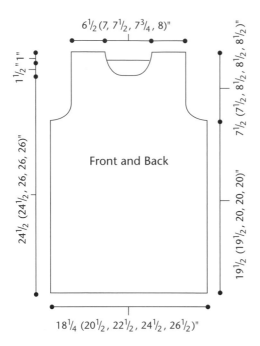

6½ (7, 7½, 7¾, 8)"

1½" 1"

Front and Back

24½ (24½, 26, 26, 26)"

7½ (7½, 8½, 8½, 8½)"

19½ (19½, 20, 20, 20)"

18¼ (20½, 22½, 24½, 26½)"

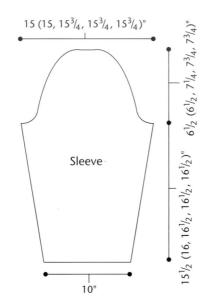

15 (15, 15¾, 15¾, 15¾)"

6½ (6½, 7¼, 7¾, 7¾)"

Sleeve

15½ (16, 16½, 16½, 16½)"

10"

Pattern Notes:

- To increase, work 2 sts into a st.
- Each sc and ch-1 sp counts as 1 st.
- For a description and illustration of any unfamiliar stitch, refer to the back of the book.

❧ Seed St Patt

Ch multiple of 2

Foundation Row (RS): Sc into second ch from hook, *ch 1, skip next ch, sc into next ch. Repeat from * across. Ch 1, turn.

Row 1 (WS): Sc into first sc, sc into next ch-1 sp, *ch 1, sc into next ch-1 sp. Repeat from * across, ending row with sc into last sc. Ch 1, turn.

Row 2: Sc into first sc, *ch 1, sc into next ch-1 sp. Repeat from * across, ending row with ch 1, sc into last sc. Ch 1, turn.

Repeat Rows 1 and 2 for patt.

❧ Sideways Rib Patt

Over any number of ch

Foundation Row: Sc into second ch from hook and into each ch across. Ch 1, turn.

Patt Row: Sc *into the back loop* of each sc across. Ch 1, turn.

Repeat Patt Row.

❧ Back

With larger hook and A, ch 88 (98, 108, 118, 128). Beg Seed St Patt, and work even on 87 (97, 107, 117, 127) sts until piece measures approx 9 (9, 9½, 9½, 9½)"/23 (23, 24, 24, 24) cm from beg, ending after WS row.

Next Row (RS): Change to B, and cont even in patt as established until piece measures approx 18 (18, 19, 19, 19)"/45.5 (45.5, 48.5, 48.5, 48.5) cm from beg, ending after WS row.

Next Row (RS): Change to C, and cont even in patt as established until piece measures approx

19½ (19½, 20, 20, 20)"/49.5 (49.5, 51, 51, 51) cm from beg, ending after WS row. *Do not ch 1 to turn.*

Shape Armholes: Next Row (RS): Slip st into first 5 (7, 9, 9, 13) sts, ch 1, dec sc to combine next sc and ch-1 sp, *ch 1, sc into next ch-1 sp. Repeat from * across until 7 (9, 11, 11, 15) sts rem in row, ending row with dec sc to combine next ch-1 sp and next sc. Ch 1, turn.

Next Row: Dec sc to combine first dec sc and next ch-1 sp, *ch 1, sc into next ch-1 sp. Repeat from * across, ending row with ch 1, dec sc to combine next ch-1 sp and last dec sc. Ch 1, turn.

Repeat last row 1 (1, 3, 5, 5) more times.

Next Row: Sc into dec sc, sc into next sc, *ch 1, sc into next ch-1 sp. Repeat from * across, ending row with sc into dec sc. Ch 1, turn.

Next Row: Dec sc to combine first 2 sc, *sc into next ch-1 sp, ch 1. Repeat from * across, ending row with dec sc to combine last 2 sc. Ch 1, turn.

Next Row: Sc into first dec sc, *ch 1, sc into next ch-1 sp. Repeat from * across, ending row with ch 1, sc into last dec sc. Ch 1, turn.

Next Row: Dec sc to combine first sc and ch-1 sp, *ch 1, sc into next ch-1 sp. Repeat from * across, ending row with ch 1, dec sc to combine next ch-1 sp and dec sc. Ch 1, turn.

Next Row: Sc into dec sc, *sc into next ch-1 sp, ch 1. Repeat from * across, ending row with sc into next ch-1 sp, sc into dec sc. Ch 1, turn—67 (73, 75, 81, 83) sts rem.

Cont even until piece measures approx 26 (26, 27½, 27½, 27½)"/66 (66, 70, 70, 70) cm from beg, ending after WS row. Ch 1, turn.

Shape Neck: Next Row (RS): Sc into first sc, *ch 1, sc into next ch-1 sp. Repeat from * 7 (8, 8,

9, 9) more times, then make an sc into next sc—18 (20, 20, 22, 22) sts. Ch 1, turn.

Next Row: Sc into first sc, *ch 1, sc into next ch-1 sp. Repeat from * across, ending row with sc into last sc.

Repeat last two rows once more. Fasten off.

For second side of neck, with RS facing, skip the middle 31 (33, 35, 37, 39) sts, join yarn with a slip st to next sc and ch 1.

Next Row (RS): Sc into same sc as slip st, *sc into next ch-1 sp, ch 1. Repeat from * across, ending row with sc into last sc. Ch 1, turn.

Next Row: Sc into first sc, *sc into next ch-1 sp, ch 1. Repeat from * across, ending row with sc into next ch-1 sp, sc into last sc. Ch 1, turn.

Repeat last two rows once more. Fasten off.

❖ Front

Work as for back until piece measures approx 24½ (24½, 26, 26, 26)"/62 (62, 66, 66, 66) cm from beg, ending after WS row. Ch 1, turn.

Shape Neck: Next Row (RS): Sc into first sc, *ch 1, sc into next ch-1 sp. Repeat from * 10 (11, 11, 12, 12) more times, ending row with sc into next sc. Ch 1, turn.

Next Row: Dec sc to combine first 2 sc, *sc into next ch-1 sp, ch 1. Repeat from * across, ending row with sc into next ch-1 sp, sc into last sc. Ch 1, turn.

Next Row: Sc into first sc, *ch 1, sc into next ch-1 sp. Repeat from * across, ending row with dec sc to combine next sc and dec sc. Ch 1, turn.

Repeat last 2 rows twice more—18 (20, 20, 22, 22) sts rem.

Cont even until piece measures same as back to shoulder. Fasten off.

For second side of neck, with RS facing, skip the middle 19 (21, 23, 25, 27) sts, join yarn with a slip st to next sc and ch 1.

Next Row (RS): Sc into same sc as slip st, *sc into next ch-1 sp, ch 1. Repeat from * across, ending row with sc into last sc. Ch 1, turn.

Next Row: Sc into first sc, *sc into next ch-1 sp, ch 1. Repeat from * across, ending row with sc into next ch-1 sp, dec sc to combine last 2 sc. Ch 1, turn.

Next Row: Dec sc to combine first dec sc and next sc, *sc into next ch-1 sp, ch 1. Repeat from * across, ending row with sc into last sc. Ch 1, turn.

Repeat last two rows twice more.

Cont even until piece measures same as back to shoulder. Fasten off.

❁ Sleeves

With larger hook and A, ch 48. Beg Seed St Patt, and work even on 47 sts for approx 1"/2.5 cm, ending after WS row. Ch 1, turn.

Next Row: 2 sc into first sc, *ch 1, sc into next ch-1 sp. Repeat from * across, ending row with ch 1, 2 sc into last sc. Ch 1, turn.

Work three rows even.

Next Row: 2 sc into first sc, *sc into next ch-1 sp, ch 1. Repeat from * across, ending row with sc into next ch-1 sp, 2 sc into last sc. Ch 1, turn.

Next Row: Sc into first 2 sc, *ch 1, sc into next ch-1 sp. Repeat from * across, ending row with ch 1, skip next sc, sc into last 2 sc. Ch 1, turn.

Work two rows even.

Repeat last eight rows 4 (4, 6, 6, 6) times—67 (67, 75, 75, 75) sts total—**and at the same time,** when piece measures approx 5 (5½, 6, 6, 6)"/12.5 (14, 15, 15, 15) cm from beg, end after WS row.

Change to B, and work even until piece measures approx 14 (14½, 15½, 15½, 15½)"/35.5 (37, 39.5, 39.5, 39.5) cm from beg, end after WS row and change to C.

For Sizes X-Small and Small Only: Next Row: 2 sc into first sc, *ch 1, sc into next ch-1 sp. Repeat from * across, ending row with ch 1, 2 sc into last sc. Ch 1, turn. Work six rows even. **Next Row:** 2 sc into first sc, *ch 1, sc into next ch-1 sp. Repeat from * across, ending row with ch 1, 2 sc into last sc—71 (71, 75, 75, 75) sts. Ch 1, turn.

For All Sizes: Cont even until sleeve measures approx 15½ (16, 16½, 16½, 16½)"/39.5 (40.5, 42, 42, 42) cm from beg, ending after WS row. *Do not ch 1 to turn.*

Shape Cap: Next Row (RS): Slip st into first 5 (7, 9, 9, 9) sts, ch 1, dec sc to combine next sc and ch-1 sp, *ch 1, sc into next ch-1 sp. Repeat from * across until 7 (9, 11, 11, 11) sts rem in row, ending row with dec sc to combine next ch-1 sp and next sc. Ch 1, turn.

Work 0 (2, 4, 4, 4) rows even in patt as established.

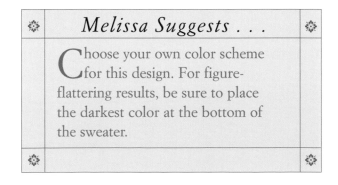

Melissa Suggests . . .

Choose your own color scheme for this design. For figure-flattering results, be sure to place the darkest color at the bottom of the sweater.

For Sizes Medium, Large, and X-Large Only:
Next Row: Sc into dec sc, *sc into next ch-1 sp,
ch 1. Repeat from * across, ending row with sc
into dec sc. Ch 1, turn. **Next Row:** Work even.
Ch 1, turn.

For Sizes Large and X-Large Only: Work two
more rows even. Ch 1, turn.

For All Sizes: Next Row (WS): Dec sc to combine
first st and next ch-1 sp, *ch 1, sc into next
ch-1 sp. Repeat from * across, ending row with
ch 1, dec sc to combine next ch-1 sp and the last
st. Ch 1, turn.

Repeat last row 24 (22, 22, 22, 22) more times—9
sts rem. Fasten off.

❈ Finishing

Sew shoulder seams.

Neckband: With RS facing, smaller hook, and C,
work 65 sc around neckline. Fasten off.

With A, ch 17. Work Sideways Rib Patt until
piece, when slightly stretched, fits around
neckline—16 sc each row. Fasten off.

Sew foundation row of neckband to the last row of
the neckband. Sewing *through back loops* of each
sc, sew neck ribbing into place in neckline, placing
seam at center of back neck.

Set in sleeves. Sew sleeve and side seams.

Variegated Summer Vest

Combine bulky hand-dyed yarn with cluster stitches to create this richly marbled piece in almost no time at all!

❀ *Sizes*

Small (Medium, Large, Extra-Large). Instructions are for smallest size, with changes for other sizes noted in parentheses as necessary.

❀ *Finished Measurements*

Bust (Buttoned): 37¼ (40, 44¼, 47)"/94.5 (101.5, 112.5, 119.5) cm
Length: 25 (26, 27, 28)"/63.5 (66, 68.5, 71) cm

❀ *Materials*

Unique Kolours/Colinette's *Wigwam* (bulky weight; 100% cotton; 3½ oz/100 g; approx 184 yd/170 m), 8 (8, 9, 10) hanks Fire #71
Crochet hook, size K/10.5 (6.50 mm) or size needed to obtain gauge
Six 1"/25 mm buttons (Zecca Button Company's *Style #811* was used on sample garment)

❀ *Gauge*

In Cluster Patt, 17 sts and 12 rows = 5"/13 cm.
To measure your gauge, make a test swatch as follows: Ch 18. Work even in Cluster Patt for 12 rows. Fasten off.
Piece should measure 5"/13 cm square. **To save time, take time to check gauge.**

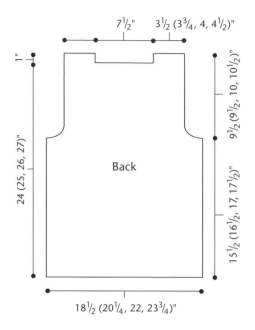

7½" 3½ (3¾, 4, 4½)"

1"

Back

24 (25, 26, 27)"

9½ (9½, 10, 10½)"

15½ (16½, 17, 17½)"

18½ (20¼, 22, 23¾)"

3½ (3¾, 4, 4½)"

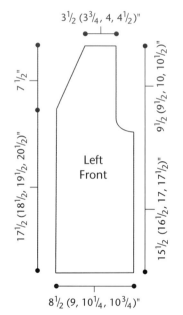

7 ½"

Left
Front

17½ (18½, 19½, 20½)"

9½ (9½, 10, 10½)"

15½ (16½, 17, 17½)"

8½ (9, 10¼, 10¾)"

Pattern Notes:

- 3-dc cluster = (Yarn over, insert hook into indicated st and pull up a loop, yarn over and draw it through 2 loops) three times, yarn over and draw it through all 4 loops on hook.
- Each sc, 3-dc cluster, ch-1 sp, and turning-ch-3 counts as 1 st.
- For even color distribution, alternate between two balls of yarn, *loosely* carrying unused yarn along side of work on WS.
- For a description and illustration of any unfamiliar stitch, refer to the back of the book.

❖ Cluster Patt

Ch multiple of 2

Foundation Row (RS): Sc into second ch from hook and into each ch across. Ch 3, turn.

Row 1 (WS): Skip first sc, *3-dc cluster into next sc, ch 1, skip next sc. Repeat from *across, ending row with 3-dc cluster into next sc, dc into last sc. Ch 1, turn.

Row 2: Sc into first dc, *sc into next 3-dc cluster, sc into next ch-1 sp. Repeat from * across, ending row with sc into next 3-dc cluster, sc into top of turning-ch-3. Ch 3, turn.

Repeat Rows 1 and 2 for patt.

❖ Back

Ch 64 (70, 76, 82). Beg Cluster Patt, and work even on 63 (69, 75, 81) sts until piece measures approx 15½ (16½, 17, 17½)"/39.5 (42, 43, 44.5) cm from beg, ending after WS row. *Do not ch 1 to turn.*

Shape Armholes: Next Row (RS): Slip st into first 3 (5, 7, 9) sts, ch 1, cont across next 57 (59, 61, 63) sts, leaving last 3 (5, 7, 9) sts unworked. Ch 3, turn.

Next Row: Skip first 2 sc, *3-dc cluster into next sc, ch 1, skip next sc. Repeat from * across, ending row with 3-dc cluster into next sc, dec dc to combine next 2 sc. Ch 1, turn.

Next Row: Dec sc to combine dec dc and next 3-dc cluster, *sc into next ch-1 sp, sc into next 3-dc cluster. Repeat from * across until 2 sts rem, ending row with dec sc to combine next 3-dc cluster and turning-ch-3. Ch 3, turn.

Repeat last two rows once more—49 (51, 53, 55) sts rem.

Cont even until piece measures approx 24 (25, 26, 27)"/61 (63.5, 66, 68.5) cm from beg, ending after WS row. Ch 1, turn.

Shape Neck: Next Row (RS): Work across first 12 (13, 14, 15) sts, ch 3, turn.

Next Row: Work even. Fasten off.

For second side of neck, with RS facing, skip the middle 25 sts, join yarn with a slip st to next st, ch 1, and complete same as first side.

❧ Left Front

Ch 30 (32, 36, 38). Beg Cluster Patt, and work even on 29 (31, 35, 37) sts until piece measures approx 15½ (16½, 17, 17½)"/39.5 (42, 43, 44.5) cm from beg, ending after WS row. *Do not ch 1 to turn.*

Shape Armhole: Dec Row 1 (RS): Slip st into first 3 (5, 7, 9) sts, ch 1, cont across to end row. Ch 3, turn.

Dec Row 2: Skip first sc, *3-dc cluster into next sc, ch 1, skip next sc. Repeat from * across, ending row with 3-dc cluster into next sc, dec dc to combine last 2 sc. Ch 1, turn.

Dec Row 3: Dec sc to combine dec dc and next 3 dc cluster, work across in patt as established to end row. Ch 3, turn.

Repeat Dec Row 2 once more—23 (23, 25, 25) sts rem.

Cont even until piece measures approx 17½ (18½, 19½, 20½)"/44.5 (47, 49.5, 52) cm from beg, ending after WS row.

Shape Neck: Next Row (RS): Work patt as established until 2 sts rem, ending row with dec sc to combine next 3-dc cluster and turning-ch-3. Ch 3, turn.

Next Row: Skip first 2 sc, *3-dc cluster into next sc, ch 1, skip next sc. Repeat from * across, ending row with 3-dc cluster into next sc, dc into last sc. Ch 1, turn.

Next Two Rows: Work same as last two rows.

Next Two Rows: Work even in Cluster Patt.

Repeat last six rows once more, then work first 3 (2, 3, 2) rows of neck shaping once more—12 (13, 14, 15) sts rem.

Cont even until piece measures same as back. Fasten off.

❧ Right Front

Work same as left front until piece measures approx 15½ (16½, 17, 17½)"/39.5 (42, 43, 44.5) cm from beg, ending after WS row. Ch 3, turn.

Shape Armhole: Dec Row 1 (RS): Work patt as established across first 26 (26, 28, 28) sts, leaving last 3 (5, 7, 9) sts unworked. Ch 3, turn.

Dec Row 2: Skip first 2 sc, *3-dc cluster into next sc, ch 1, skip next sc. Repeat from * across, ending row with 3-dc cluster into next sc, dc into last sc. Ch 1, turn.

Dec Row 3: Work patt as established until 2 sts rem, ending row with dec sc to combine next 3 dc cluster and turning-ch-3. Ch 3, turn.

Repeat Dec Row 2 once more—23 (23, 25, 25) sts rem.

Cont even until piece measures approx 17½ (18½, 19½, 20½)"/44.5 (47, 49.5, 52) cm from beg, ending after WS row. Ch 1, turn.

Shape Neck: Next Row (RS): Dec sc to combine first dc and next 3-dc cluster, *sc into next ch-1 sp, sc into next 3-dc cluster. Repeat from *

across, ending row with sc into top of turning-ch-3. Ch 3, turn.

Next Row: Skip first sc, *3-dc cluster into next sc, ch 1, skip next sc. Repeat from * across, ending row with 3-dc cluster into next sc, dec dc to combine last 2 sc. Ch 1, turn.

Next Two Rows: Work same as last two rows.

Next Two Rows: Work even in Cluster Patt.

Repeat last six rows once more, then work first 3 (2, 3, 2) rows of neck shaping once more—12 (13, 14, 15) sts rem.

Cont even until piece measures same as back. Fasten off.

❖ Finishing

Sew shoulder seams.

Front Bands: With RS facing, attach yarn with a slip st to lower right front edge and ch 1. Work rows of sc along right front edge, around neckline, and down left front edge until band measures approx ¾"/2 cm from beg, working 2 sc at beg of each front neck shaping and working dec sc at beg of each back neck shaping.

Place markers for six evenly spaced buttons along left front, making the first ½"/1.5 cm from bottom edge and the last ¼"/0.5 cm from beg of front neck shaping.

Next Row: Cont in sc as before, and make six buttonholes along right front by working (ch 3, skip next 3 sc) opposite markers.

Next Row: Cont in sc as before, and work 3 sc into each ch-3 sp.

Cont in sc as before until band measures approx 1¾"/4.5 cm from beg. Fasten off.

Sew side seams.

Armhole Bands: With RS facing, attach yarn with a slip st to side seam and ch 1. Work three rnds of sc around armhole. Fasten off.

Sew on buttons.

Fisherman-Style Pullover

Here's a crocheter's spin on a traditional Aran design. The engaging mix of patterns yields a warm, easy-fitting classic.

ADVANCED

❀ *Sizes*

Small (Medium, Large, Extra-Large). Instructions are for smallest size, with changes for other sizes noted in parentheses as necessary.

Finished Measurements

Bust: 41 (44, 47, 50)"/104 (112, 119.5, 127) cm
Length: 27 (28, 28, 29)"/68.5 (71, 71, 73.5) cm
Sleeve width at underarm: 18 (19, 20, 21)"/45.5 (48.5, 51, 53.5) cm

❀ *Materials*

Lion Brand's *Wool-Ease* (worsted weight; 80% acrylic/20% wool; 3 oz/85 g; approx 197 yd/177 m), 12 (13, 14, 15) skeins Fisherman #99
Crochet hooks, sizes G/6 and H/8 (4.25 and 5.00 mm) or size needed to obtain gauge

❀ *Gauge*

With larger hook in Fisherman's Patt, 16 sts and 15 rows = 4"/10 cm.
With larger hook in solid hdc, 17 hdc and 11 rows = 4"/10 cm.
To measure your gauge, make a test swatch as follows: With larger hook, ch 18.
Foundation Row: Hdc into third ch from hook and into each ch across. Ch 2, turn.
  Next Row: Skip first hdc, hdc into each hdc across, ending row with hdc into top of turning-ch-2. Ch 2, turn.
Repeat last row nine more times. Fasten off.
Piece should measure 4"/10 cm square. **To save time, take time to check gauge.**

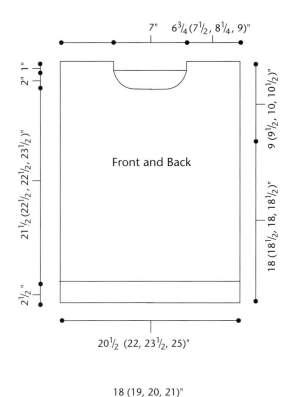

Pattern Notes:

- Bobble = 5 dc into indicated st, drop loop from hook; insert hook from front to back into first dc made, replace loop onto hook and draw loop through.

- C5R (cross 5 sts to the right) = *Skip next 3 sts*, FPDTR into next 2 FPTR two rows below; skip the 2 hdc behind the last FPTR just made; working on the skipped sts between the *'s make 1 hdc in third hdc; working between the last 2 FPDTR just made and the main fabric, make 1 FPDTR into the first and then also into the second FPTR two rows below.

- C5L (cross 5 sts to the left) = Skip next 3 sts, FPDTR into next 2 FPTR two rows below; skip 2 sts behind the FPDTR just made; hdc into next hdc, working in front of the last 2 FPDTR just made, make 1 FPDTR into the first and then the second skipped FPTR two rows below.

- C4R (cross 4 sts to the right) = Skip next 2 sts, FPDTR into next 2 FPTR two rows below; working between the last 2 FPDTR just made and the main fabric, make 1 FPDTR into the first and then the second skipped FPTR two rows below.

- C4L (cross 4 sts to the left) = Skip next 2 FPSTS, FPDTR into next 2 FPTR two rows below; working in front of the last 2 FPDTR just made, make 1 FPDTR into the first and then also into the second skipped FPTR two rows below.

- Each turning-ch-2 counts as 1 hdc.

- To decrease in hdc, work until 2 sts rem in row, then work a dec hdc to combine the last 2 sts in row. On the next row, work the last st into the last hdc, *not into the top of the turning-ch-2.*

- To increase, work 2 sts into a st.

- For a description and illustration of any unfamiliar stitch, refer to the back of the book.

Front and Back

7"   6¾ (7½, 8¼, 9)"

2" 1"

9 (9½, 10, 10½)"

21½ (22½, 22½, 23½)"

18 (18½, 18, 18½)"

2½"

20½ (22, 23½, 25)"

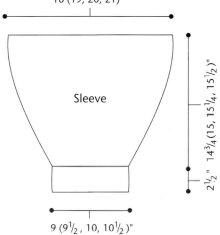

Sleeve

18 (19, 20, 21)"

14¾ (15, 15¼, 15½)"

2½"

9 (9½, 10, 10½)"

✿ Sideways Rib Patt

Over any number of ch

Foundation Row: Sc into second ch from hook and into each ch across. Ch 1, turn.

Patt Row: Sc *into the back loop* of each sc across. Ch 1, turn.

Repeat Patt Row.

❧ Back

With smaller hook, ch 13. Work Sideways Rib Patt on 12 sts for 82 (88, 94, 100) rows. Ch 2, work 81 (87, 93, 99) hdc evenly along the long edge of rib. Change to larger hook, ch 2, turn, and establish Fisherman's Patt as follows.

Row 1 (RS): Skip first hdc, hdc into next 3 hdc, *FPTR into next 2 hdc, skip 2 hdc behind the 2 FPTR just made, hdc into next 3 hdc, FPTR into next 2 hdc, skip 2 hdc behind the 2 FPTR just made, hdc into next 1 (2, 3, 4) hdc, (FPTR into next 2 hdc, skip 2 hdc behind the 2 FPTR just made, hdc into next hdc) twice, FPTR into next 2 hdc, skip 2 hdc behind the 2 FPTR just made, hdc into next 1 (2, 3, 4) hdc, FPTR into next 2 hdc, skip 2 hdc behind the 2 FPTR just made, hdc into next 3 hdc, FPTR into next 2 hdc, skip 2 hdc behind the 2 FPTR just made**, hdc into next 1 (2, 3, 4) hdc, FPTR into next 2 hdc, skip 2 hdc behind the 2 FPTR just made, (hdc into next 4 hdc, FPTR into next 4 hdc, skip 4 hdc behind the 4 FPTR just made) twice, hdc into next 4 hdc, FPTR into next 2 hdc, skip 2 hdc behind the 2 FPTR just made, hdc into next 1 (2, 3, 4) hdc. Repeat from * to ** once more, then work hdc into next 3 hdc, hdc into top of turning-ch-2. Ch 2, turn.

Row 2 and All WS Rows: Skip first hdc, hdc into each st across, ending row with hdc into top of turning-ch-2. Ch 2, turn.

Row 3: Skip first hdc, hdc into next 3 hdc, *FPTR into next 2 FPSTS two rows below, skip 2 hdc behind the 2 FPTR just made, hdc into next hdc, Bobble into next hdc, hdc into next hdc, FPTR into next 2 FPSTS two rows below, skip 2 hdc behind the 2 FPTR just made, hdc into next 1 (2, 3, 4) hdc, C5R, skip 2 hdc behind the last 2 FPDTR just made, hdc into next hdc, FPTR into next 2 FPSTS two rows below, skip 2 hdc behind

the 2 FPTR just made, hdc into next 1 (2, 3, 4) hdc, FPTR into next 2 FPSTS two rows below, skip 2 hdc behind the 2 FPTR just made, hdc into next hdc, Bobble into next hdc, hdc into next hdc, FPTR into next 2 FPSTS two rows below, skip 2 hdc behind the 2 FPTR just made**; for center panel, [skip next 2 FPTR, hdc into next 2 (3, 4, 5) hdc, (FPDTR into 2 skipped FPSTS two rows below, skip 2 hdc behind the 2 FPDTR just made, hdc into next 2 hdc, FPDTR into next 2 FPSTS two rows below, skip 2 hdc behind the 2 FPDTR just made, skip next 2 FPSTS, hdc into next 2 hdc) twice, FPDTR into 2 skipped FPSTS two rows below, skip 2 hdc behind the 2 FPDTR just made, hdc into next 2 hdc, FPDTR into next 2 FPSTS two rows below, skip 2 hdc behind the 2 FPDTR just made, hdc into next 2 (3, 4, 5) hdc.] Repeat from * to ** once more, then work hdc into next 3 hdc, hdc into top of turning-ch-2. Ch 2, turn.

Row 5: Skip first hdc, hdc into next 3 hdc, *FPTR into next 2 FPTR two rows below, skip 2 hdc behind the 2 FPTR just made, hdc into next 3 hdc, FPTR into next 2 FPTR two rows below, skip 2 hdc behind the 2 FPTR just made, hdc into next 1 (2, 3, 4) hdc, FPTR into next 2 FPDTR two rows below, skip 2 hdc behind the 2 FPTR just made, hdc into next hdc, C5L, skip 2 hdc behind the 2 FPDTR just made, hdc into next 1 (2, 3, 4) hdc, FPTR into next 2 FPTR, skip 2 hdc behind the

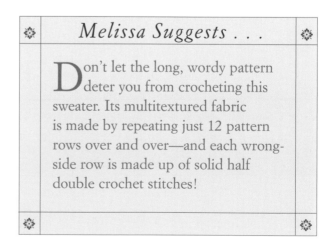

Melissa Suggests . . .

Don't let the long, wordy pattern deter you from crocheting this sweater. Its multitextured fabric is made by repeating just 12 pattern rows over and over—and each wrong-side row is made up of solid half double crochet stitches!

2 FPTR just made, hdc into next 3 hdc, FPTR into next 2 FPTR, skip 2 hdc behind the 2 FPTR just made**, skip next 2 FPSTS, hdc into next 3 (4, 5, 6) hdc, (FPDTR into skipped 2 FPDTR two rows below, FPDTR into next 2 FPDTR two rows below, skip 4 hdc behind the 4 FPDTR just made, hdc into next 4 hdc) twice, FPDTR into skipped 2 FPDTR two rows below, FPDTR into next 2 FPDTR two rows below, skip 4 hdc behind the 4 FPDTR just made, hdc into next 3 (4, 5, 6) hdc. Repeat from * to ** once more, ending row with hdc into next 3 hdc, hdc into top of turning-ch-2. Ch 2, turn.

Row 7: Skip first hdc, hdc into next 3 hdc, *FPTR into next 2 FPTR two rows below, skip 2 hdc behind the 2 FPTR just made, hdc into next 3 hdc, FPTR into next 2 FPTR two rows below, skip 2 hdc behind the 2 FPTR just made, hdc into next 1 (2, 3, 4) hdc, C5R, skip 2 hdc behind the last 2 FPDTR just made, hdc into next hdc, FPTR into next 2 FPDTR two rows below, hdc into next 1 (2, 3, 4) hdc, FPTR into next 2 FPTR two rows below, skip 2 hdc behind the 2 FPTR just made, hdc into next 3 hdc, FPTR into next 2 FPTR two rows below, skip 2 hdc behind the 2 FPTR just made**, hdc into next 3 (4, 5, 6) hdc, (C4L, skip 4 hdc behind the 4 FPDTR just made, hdc into next 4 hdc) twice, C4L, skip 4 hdc behind the 4 FPDTR just made, hdc into next 3 (4, 5, 6) hdc. Repeat from * to ** once more, ending row with hdc into next 3 hdc, hdc into top of turning-ch-2. Ch 2, turn.

Row 9: Skip first hdc, hdc into next 3 hdc, *FPTR into next 2 FPTR two rows below, skip 2 hdc behind the 2 FPTR just made, hdc into next hdc, Bobble into next hdc, hdc into next hdc, FPTR into next 2 FPTR two rows below, skip 2 hdc behind the 2 FPTR just made, hdc into next 1 (2, 3, 4) hdc, FPTR into next 2 FPDTR two rows below, skip 2 hdc behind the 2 FPTR just made,

hdc into next hdc, C5L, skip 2 hdc behind the last 2 FPDTR just made, hdc into next 1 (2, 3, 4) hdc, FPTR into next 2 FPTR two rows below, skip 2 hdc behind the 2 FPTR just made, hdc into next hdc, Bobble into next hdc, hdc into next hdc, FPTR into next 2 FPTR two rows below, skip 2 hdc behind the 2 FPTR just made**, hdc into next 2 (3 4, 5) hdc, (FPDTR into next 2 FPDTR two rows below, skip 2 hdc behind the 2 FPDTR just made, hdc into next 2 hdc, FPDTR into next 2 FPDTR two rows below, skip 2 hdc behind the 2 FPDTR just made, hdc into next 2 hdc) twice, FPDTR into next 2 FPDTR two rows below, skip 2 hdc behind the 2 FPDTR just made, hdc into next 2 hdc, FPDTR into next 2 FPDTR two rows below, skip 2 hdc behind the 2 FPDTR just made, hdc into next 2 (3, 4, 5) hdc. Repeat from * to ** once more, ending row with hdc into next 3 hdc, hdc into top of turning-ch-2. Ch 2, turn.

Row 11: Skip first hdc, hdc into next 3 hdc, *FPTR into next 2 FPTR two rows below, skip 2 hdc behind the 2 FPTR just made, hdc into next 3 hdc, FPTR into next 2 FPTR two rows below, skip 2 hdc behind the 2 FPTR just made, hdc into next 1 (2, 3, 4) hdc, C5R, skip 2 hdc behind the last 2 FPDTR just made, hdc into next hdc, FPTR into next 2 FPDTR two rows below, hdc into next 1 (2, 3, 4) hdc, FPTR into next 2 FPTR two rows below, skip 2 hdc behind the 2 FPTR just made, hdc into next 3 hdc, FPTR into next 2 FPTR two rows below, skip 2 hdc behind the 2 FPTR just made**, hdc into next 1 (2, 3, 4) hdc, FPDTR into next 2 FPDTR two rows below, skip 2 hdc behind the 2 FPDTR just made, (hdc into next 4 hdc, FPDTR into next 2 FPDTR two rows below, FPDTR into next 2 FPDTR two rows below, skip 4 hdc behind the 4 FPDTR just made) twice, hdc into next 4 hdc, FPDTR into next 2 FPDTR two rows below, skip 2 hdc behind the 2 FPDTR just made, hdc into next 1 (2, 3, 4) hdc. Repeat from *

to ** once more, ending row with hdc into next 3 hdc, hdc into top of turning-ch-2. Ch 2, turn.

Row 13: Skip first hdc, hdc into next 3 hdc, *FPTR into next 2 FPTR, skip 2 hdc behind the 2 FPTR just made, hdc into next 3 hdc, FPTR into next 2 FPTR two rows below, skip 2 hdc behind the 2 FPTR just made, hdc into next 1 (2, 3, 4) hdc, FPTR into next 2 FPDTR two rows below, skip 2 hdc behind the 2 FPTR just made, hdc into next hdc, C5L, skip 2 hdc behind the 2 FPDTR just made, hdc into next 1 (2, 3, 4) hdc, FPTR into next 2 FPTR two rows below, skip 2 hdc behind the 2 FPTR just made, hdc into next 3 hdc, FPTR into next 2 FPTR two rows below, skip 2 hdc behind the 2 FPTR just made**, hdc into next 1 (2, 3, 4) hdc, FPTR into next 2 FPDTR two rows below, skip 2 hdc behind the 2 FPTR just made, (hdc into next 4 hdc, C4R, skip 4 hdc behind the 4 FPDTR just made) twice, hdc into next 4 hdc, FPTR into next 2 FPDTR two rows below, skip 2 hdc behind the 2 FPTR just made, hdc into next 1 (2, 3, 4) hdc. Repeat from * to ** once more, ending row with hdc into next 3 hdc, hdc into top of turning-ch-2. Ch 2, turn.

Row 14: Work same as Row 2.

Repeat Rows 3–14 for patt until piece measures approx 26 (27, 27, 28)"/66 (68.5, 68.5, 71) cm from beg, ending after WS row. Ch 2, turn.

Shape Neck: Next Row (RS): Skip first hdc, work in patt as established across next 26 (29, 32, 35) sts, ch 2, turn, leaving rest of row unworked.

Cont even until this side measures approx 27 (28, 28, 29)"/68.5 (71, 71, 73.5) cm from beg. Fasten off.

For second side of neck, with RS facing, skip the middle 28 sts and attach yarn with a slip st to next st and ch 2. Complete as for first side.

✿ Front

Work as for back until piece measures approx 24 (25, 25, 26)"/61 (63.5, 63.5, 66) cm from beg, ending after WS row. Ch 2, turn.

Shape Neck: Next Row (RS): Skip first hdc, cont in patt across next 32 (35, 38, 41) sts, ch 2, turn.

Dec 1 st at neck edge every row six times, then work even until this side measures same as back. Fasten off.

For second side of neck, with RS facing, skip the middle 16 sts and attach yarn with a slip st to next st and ch 2. Complete as for first side.

✿ Sleeves

With smaller hook, ch 13. Work Sideways Rib Patt on 12 sts for 36 (38, 40, 42) rows. Ch 2, work 35 (37, 39, 41) hdc evenly along the long edge of rib. Change to larger hook, ch 2, turn, and establish Fisherman's Patt as follows.

Row 1 (RS): Skip first hdc, hdc into next 2 hdc, FPTR into next 2 hdc, skip 2 hdc behind the 2 FPTR just made, hdc into next 1 (2, 3, 4) hdc, FPTR into next 2 hdc, skip 2 hdc behind the 2 FPTR just made, (hdc into next 4 hdc, FPTR into next 4 hdc, skip 4 hdc behind the 4 FPTR just made) twice, hdc into next 4 hdc, FPTR into next 2 hdc, skip 2 hdc behind the 2 FPTR just made, hdc into next 1 (2, 3, 4) hdc, FPTR into next 2 hdc, skip 2 hdc behind the 2 FPTR just made, hdc into next 2 hdc, hdc into top of turning-ch-2. Ch 2, turn.

Row 2 and All WS Rows: Skip first hdc, hdc into each st across, ending row with hdc into top of turning-ch-2. Ch 2, turn.

Row 3: Skip first hdc, Bobble into next hdc, hdc into next hdc, FPTR into next 2 FPSTS two rows

below, skip 2 hdc behind the 2 FPTR just made; for center panel, [skip next 2 FPSTS, hdc into next 2 (3, 4, 5) hdc, (FPDTR into 2 skipped FPSTS two rows below, skip 2 hdc behind the 2 FPDTR just made, hdc into next 2 hdc, FPDTR into next 2 FPSTS two rows below, skip 2 hdc behind the 2 FPDTR just made, skip next 2 FPSTS, hdc into next 2 hdc) twice, FPDTR into 2 skipped FPSTS two rows below, skip 2 hdc behind the 2 FPDTR just made, hdc into next 2 hdc, FPDTR into next 2 FPSTS two rows below, skip 2 hdc behind the 2 FPDTR just made, hdc into next 2 (3, 4, 5) hdc], FPTR into next 2 FPSTS two rows below, skip 2 hdc behind the 2 FPTR just made, hdc into next hdc, Bobble into next hdc, hdc into top of turning-ch-2. Ch 2, turn.

Cont in patt as established, and inc 1 st each side every other row 16 (17, 19, 20) times, then every fourth row 2 (2, 1, 1) times, working new sts into Fisherman's Patt same as back—72 (76, 80, 84) sts.

Cont even until sleeve measures approx 17¼ (17½, 17¾, 18)"/44 (44.5, 45, 45.5) cm from beg. Fasten off.

✷ Finishing

Sew shoulder seams.

Neckband: With smaller hook and RS facing, work 76 sc around neckline. Fasten off.

With smaller hook, ch 7. Work Sideways Rib Patt until piece, when slightly stretched, fits around neckline—6 sc each row. Fasten off.

Sew foundation row of neckband to the last row of the neckband. Sewing *through back loops* of each sc, sew neck ribbing into place in neckline, placing seam at center of back neck.

Place markers 9 (9½, 10, 10½)"/23 (24, 25.5, 26.5) cm down from shoulders. Set in sleeves between markers. Sew sleeve and side seams.

Delicate Summer Jacket

Take a mélange of stitches and create this elegant and versatile piece that's sure to be an instant favorite!

❀ *Sizes*

Small (Medium, Large, Extra-Large). Instructions are for smallest size, with changes for other sizes noted in parentheses as necessary.

❀ *Finished Measurements*

Bust (Buttoned): 36¾ (42¼, 47½, 52½)"/93.5 (107.5, 120.5, 133.5) cm
Length (Including Edging): 21 (21, 24¾, 24¾)"/53.5 (53.5, 63, 63) cm
Sleeve width at upper arm: 18 (18, 19½, 19½)"/45.5 (45.5, 49.5,
    49.5) cm

❀ *Materials*

Coats and Clark's *Lustersheen* (fingering weight; 100% acrylic; 1⅘ oz/51.5 g;
    approx 150 yd/135 m), 14 (15, 16, 17) balls White #1
Crochet hooks, sizes D/3 and E/4 (3.25 and 3.50 mm) or size needed to obtain
    gauge
Three ½"/13 mm buttons (JHB International's *Munich Style #37089* in White was
    used on sample garment)

❀ *Gauge*

In patt with larger hook, 25 dc = 4"/10 cm wide and 10 rows − 3"/7.5 cm long.
To measure your gauge, make a test swatch as follows: With larger hook, ch 35.
    Work Delicate Lace Patt for 10 rows. Fasten off.
Piece should measure 5¼"/13.5 cm wide and 3"/7.5 cm long. **To save time, take
    time to check gauge.**

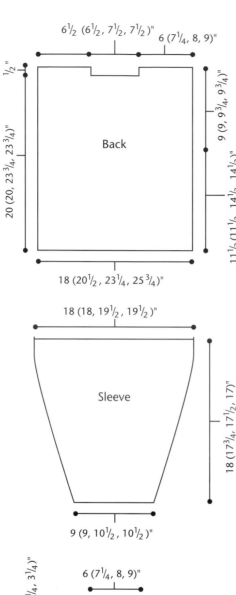

6¹/₂ (6¹/₂, 7¹/₂, 7¹/₂)"   6 (7¹/₄, 8, 9)"

¹/₂"

Back

20 (20, 23³/₄, 23³/₄)"

9 (9, 9³/₄, 9³/₄)"

11¹/₂ (11¹/₂, 14¹/₂, 14¹/₂)"

18 (20¹/₂, 23¹/₄, 25 ³/₄)"

18 (18, 19¹/₂, 19¹/₂)"

Sleeve

18 (17³/₄, 17¹/₂, 17)"

9 (9, 10¹/₂, 10¹/₂)"

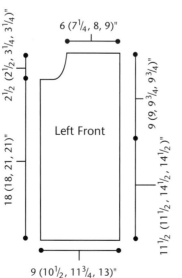

6 (7¹/₄, 8, 9)"

2¹/₂ (2¹/₂, 3¹/₄, 3¹/₄)"

9 (9, 9³/₄, 9³/₄)"

Left Front

18 (18, 21, 21)"

11¹/₂ (11¹/₂, 14¹/₂, 14¹/₂)"

9 (10¹/₂, 11³/₄, 13)"

Note: These measurements do not include the edging.

- 4-dc cluster = (Yarn over, insert hook into indicated st and pull up a loop, yarn over and draw it through 2 loops) four times, yarn over and draw it through all 5 loops on hook.

- 3-dc cluster = (Yarn over, insert hook into indicated st and pull up a loop, yarn over and draw it through 2 loops) three times, yarn over and draw it through all 4 loops on hook.

- For a description and illustration of any un-familiar stitch, refer to the back of the book.

❀ *Delicate Lace Patt*

Ch multiple of 8 + 3

Foundation Row (RS): Dc into fourth ch from hook and into each ch across. Ch 1, turn.

Row 1 (WS): Sc into first 2 dc, *4-dc cluster into next dc, sc into next 3 dc. Repeat from * across, ending row with 4-dc cluster into next dc, sc into next dc, sc into top of turning-ch-3. Ch 3, turn.

Row 2: Skip first sc, *dc into each st across. Repeat from * across. Ch 4, turn.

Row 3: Skip first 2 dc, *dc into next dc, ch 1, skip next dc. Repeat from * across, ending row with dc into top of turning-ch-3. Ch 3, turn.

Row 4: Skip first dc, *dc into next ch-1 sp, dc into next dc. Repeat from * across, ending row with dc under turning-ch-4, dc into third ch of turning-ch. Ch 5, turn.

Row 5: Skip first 2 dc, *sc into next dc, ch 5, skip next 3 dc. Repeat from * across, ending row with sc into next dc, ch 2, skip next dc, dc into top of turning-ch-3. Ch 1, turn.

Row 6: Sc into first dc, *(3 dc, ch 1, 3 dc) into next ch-5 sp, sc into next ch-5 sp. Repeat from * across, ending row with (3 dc, ch 1, 3 dc) into next ch-5 sp, sc under turning-ch-5. Ch 6, turn.

Row 7: *Sc into next ch-1 sp, ch 3, dc into next sc, ch 3. Repeat from * across, ending row with sc into next ch-1 sp, ch 3, dc into last sc. Ch 3, turn.

Row 8: Skip first dc, *3 dc into next ch-3 sp, dc into next st. Repeat from * across, ending row with 3 dc under turning-ch-6, dc into third ch of turning-ch. Ch 4, turn.

Row 9: Skip first 2 dc, *dc into next dc, ch 1, skip next dc. Repeat from * across, ending row with dc into top of turning-ch-3. Ch 3, turn.

Row 10: Skip first dc, *dc into next ch-1 sp, dc into next dc. Repeat from * across, ending row with dc under turning-ch-4, dc into third ch of turning-ch. Ch 1, turn.

Repeat Rows 1–10 for patt.

❀ Back

With larger hook, ch 115 (131, 147, 163). Beg Delicate Lace Patt, and work even on 113 (129, 145, 161) sts until piece measures approx 20 (20, 23¾, 23¾)"/51 (51, 60.5, 60.5) cm from beg, ending after Row 1 (Row 1, Row 3, Row 3) of patt. Ch 3, turn.

Shape Neck for Sizes Small and Medium Only: Next Row (RS): Skip first sc, dc into next 36 (44) sts. Fasten off, leaving rest of row unworked. For second side of neck, with RS facing, skip the middle 39 sts and attach yarn with a slip st to next st and ch 3. Work dc into next 36 (44) sts. Fasten off.

Shape Neck for Sizes Large and X-Large Only: Next Row (RS): Skip first dc, (dc into next ch-1 sp, dc into next dc) 24 (28) times. Fasten off, leaving rest of row unworked. For second side of neck, with RS facing and larger hook, skip the middle 24 ch-1 spaces and attach yarn with a slip st to next dc and ch 3. Work (dc into next ch-1 sp, dc into next dc) 24 (28) times. Fasten off.

❀ Left Front

With larger hook, ch 59 (67, 75, 83). Beg Delicate Lace Patt, and work even on 57 (65, 73, 81) sts until piece measures approx 18 (18, 21, 21)"/45.5 (45.5, 53.5, 53.5) cm from beg, ending after Row 4 of patt. *Do not ch 5 to turn.*

Shape Neck: Next Row (WS): Slip st into first 9 dc, ch 5, skip next dc, *sc into next dc, ch 5, skip next 3 dc. Repeat from * across, ending row with sc into next dc, ch 2, dc into top of turning-ch-3. Ch 1, turn.

Next Row: Sc into first dc, *(3 dc, ch 1, 3 dc) into next ch-5 sp, sc into next ch-5 sp. Repeat from * across, ending row with (3 dc, ch 1, 3 dc) into next ch-5 sp, slip st under turning-ch-5. Ch 4, turn.

Next Row: Slip st into first ch-1 sp, ^ch 3, dc into next sc, ch 3, sc into next ch-1 sp. Repeat from * across, ending row with ch 3, dc into last sc. Ch 3, turn.

Next Row: Skip first dc, *3 dc into next ch-3 sp, dc into next st. Repeat from * across, ending row with 3 dc into next ch-3 sp, dec dc to combine next dc and sc. Ch 4, turn.

Next Row: Skip first dec dc and the next dc, *dc into next dc, ch 1, skip next dc. Repeat from * across, ending row with dc into top of turning-ch-3. Ch 3, turn.

Next Row: Skip first dc, *dc into next ch-1 sp, dc into next dc. Repeat from * across, ending row with dec dc to combine next ch-1 sp and dec dc. Ch 1, turn.

Next Row: Dec sc to combine first dec dc and the next dc, sc into next dc, *4-dc cluster into next dc, sc into next 3 dc. Repeat from * across, ending row with 4-dc cluster into next dc, sc into next sc, sc into top of turning-ch-3. Ch 3, turn.

Next Row: Skip first sc, *dc into next st. Repeat from * across until 2 sts rem in row, ending row with dec dc to combine the last 2 sts in row.

For Sizes Small and Medium Only: Fasten off.

For Sizes Large and X-Large Only: Cont as follows: Ch 4, turn.

Next Row: Skip first dec dc and the next dc, dec dc to combine the next 2 dc, *ch 1, skip next dc, dc into next dc. Repeat from * across, ending row with ch 1, skip next dc, dc into top of turning-ch-3. Ch 3, turn.

Next Row: Skip first dc, *dc into next ch-1 sp, dc into next dc. Repeat from * across, ending row with dc into next ch-1 sp, dc into dec dc. Fasten off.

❧ Right Front

Work same as left front until piece measures approx 18 (18, 21, 21)"/45.5 (45.5, 53.5, 53.5) cm from beg, ending after Row 4 of patt. Ch 5, turn.

Shape Neck: Next Row (WS): Work same as Row 5 of Delicate Lace Patt until 8 sts rem in row. Ch 1, turn, leaving rest of row unworked.

Next Row: *(3 dc, ch 1, 3 dc) into next ch-5 sp, sc into next ch-5 sp. Repeat from * across, ending row with (3 dc, ch 1, 3 dc) into next ch-5 sp, sc into third ch of turning-ch-5. Ch 6, turn.

Next Row: *Sc into next ch-1 sp, ch 3, dc into next sc, ch 3. Repeat from * across, ending row with slip st into last ch-1 sp. Ch 3, turn.

Next Row: Dc into next dc, *3 dc into next ch-3 sp, dc into next st. Repeat from * across, ending

row with 3 dc under turning-ch-6, dc into third ch of turning-ch. Ch 4, turn.

Next Row: Skip first 2 dc, *dc into next dc, ch 1, skip next dc. Repeat from * across, ending row with dec dc to combine next dc and top of dec dc. Ch 3, turn.

Next Row: Skip dec dc, dec dc to combine first ch-1 sp and next dc, *dc into next dc, dc into next ch-1 sp. Repeat from * across, ending row with dc into next dc, dc under turning-ch-4, dc into third ch of turning-ch. Ch 1, turn.

Next Row: Sc into first 2 dc, *4-dc cluster into next dc, sc into next 3 dc. Repeat from * across, ending row with 4-dc cluster into next dc, dec sc to combine next 2 dc. Ch 3, turn.

Next Row: Skip dec sc, *dc into next st. Repeat from * across.

For Sizes Small and Medium Only: Fasten off.

For Sizes Large and X-Large Only: Cont as follows: Ch 4, turn.

Next Row: Skip first 2 dc, dc into next dc, *ch 1, skip next dc, dc into next dc. Repeat from * across, ending row with ch 1, skip next dc, dec dc to combine next 2 dc, ch 1, dc into last dc. Ch 3, turn.

Next Row: Skip first dc, *dc into next ch-1 sp, dc into next dc. Repeat from * across, ending row with dc under turning-ch-4, dc into third ch of turning-ch. Fasten off.

❧ Sleeves

With larger hook, ch 59 (59, 67, 67). Beg Delicate Lace Patt, and work even on 57 (57, 65, 65) sts for two rows total. Ch 3, turn.

Inc Row 1: Dc into first sc, *dc into next st. Repeat from * across, ending row with 2 dc into last sc. Ch 4, turn.

Inc Row 2: Skip first dc, *dc into next dc, ch 1, skip next dc. Repeat from * across, ending row with dc into next dc, ch 1, dc into top of turning-ch-3. Ch 3, turn.

Inc Row 3: Dc into first dc, *dc into next ch-1 sp, dc into next dc. Repeat from * across, ending row with dc under turning-ch-4, 2 dc into third ch of turning-ch. Ch 5, turn.

Inc Row 4: Skip first dc, *sc into next dc, ch 5, skip next 3 sc. Repeat from * across, ending row with sc into next dc, ch 2, dc into top of turning-ch-3. Ch 1, turn.

Inc Row 5: Sc into first dc, *(3 dc, ch 1, 3 dc) into next ch-5 sp, sc into next ch-5 sp. Repeat from * across, ending row with (3 dc, ch 1, 3 dc) into next ch-5 sp, sc under turning-ch-5. Ch 6, turn.

Inc Row 6: *Sc into next ch-1 sp, ch 3, dc into next sc, ch 3. Repeat from * across, ending row with sc into next ch-1 sp, ch 3, dc into last sc. Ch 3, turn.

Inc Row 7: Dc into first dc, *3 dc into next ch-3 sp, dc into next st. Repeat from * across, ending row with 3 dc under turning-ch-6, 2 dc into third ch of turning-ch. Ch 4, turn.

Inc Row 8: Skip first dc, *dc into next dc, ch 1, skip next dc. Repeat from * across, ending row with dc into next dc, ch 1, dc into third ch of turning-ch-3. Ch 3, turn.

Inc Row 9: Dc into first dc, *dc into next ch-1 sp, dc into next dc. Repeat from * across, ending row with dc under turning-ch-4, 2 dc into third ch of turning-ch. Ch 1, turn.

Inc Row 10: 2 sc into first dc, *4-dc cluster into next dc, sc into next 3 dc. Repeat from * across, ending row with 4-dc cluster into next dc, 2 sc into top of turning-ch-3. Ch 3, turn.

Repeat Inc Rows 1–10 once more.

Work 10 rows even.

Repeat Inc Rows 1–10 once more.

Work Inc Rows 1–6 once.

Work even on 113 (113, 121, 121) sts until sleeve measures approx 18 (17¾, 17½, 17)"/45.5 (45, 44.5, 43) cm from beg. Fasten off.

❧ Finishing

Back Lower Edging: With RS facing and smaller hook, attach yarn with a slip st to first ch of foundation ch on back and ch 4.

Row 1 (RS): Working along opposite side of foundation ch, skip first 2 ch, *sc into next ch, ch 3, skip next 2 ch, sc into next ch, ch 5, skip next 4 ch. Repeat from * across, ending row with sc into next ch, ch 3, skip next 2 ch, sc into next ch, ch 2, dc into last ch. Ch 1, turn.

Row 2: Sc into first dc, *ch 3, 3 dc into next ch-3 sp, ch 3, sc into next ch-5 sp. Repeat from * across, ending row with ch 3, 3 dc into next ch-3 sp, ch 3, sc under turning-ch-4. Ch 4, turn.

Row 3: *3-dc cluster over next 3 dc, ch 3, slip st into top of 3-dc cluster just made, ch 4, sc into next sc, ch 4. Repeat from * across, ending row with 3-dc cluster over next 3 dc, ch 3, slip st into top of 3-dc cluster just made, ch 4, sc into last sc. Fasten off.

Left Front, Right Front, and Sleeve Bottom Edging: Work as for back lower edging.

Sew shoulder seams.

Place markers 9 (9, 9¾, 9¾)"/23 (23, 25, 25) cm down from shoulders. Set in sleeves between markers. Sew sleeve and side seams.

Melissa Suggests . . .

If you would prefer to have your jacket button all the way up the front, simply place markers for 6 (6, 7, 7) evenly spaced buttonholes along the right front, making the first one ¼"/0.5 cm down from neck edge and the last one ¼"/0.5 cm from the bottom edge. Complete as directed in the pattern, making chain-three buttonholes where marked.

Front Bands: With RS facing and smaller hook, attach yarn with a slip st to lower right front edge and ch 1.

Row 1 (RS): Work 244 (244, 284, 284) sc along right front, across back of neck and down left front, working dec sc each side at beg of back neck shaping and 3 sc at beg of front neck shaping. Ch 1, turn.

Row 2: Sc into each sc, working dec sc each side at beg of back neck shaping and 3 sc at beg of front neck shaping. Ch 1, turn.

Place markers for three buttonholes along right front, making the first one ¼"/0.5 cm down from neck edge, the last one 4½"/11.5 cm down from the first, and the middle one evenly spaced between the first two.

Next Row: Work same as last row, *except* work three buttonholes by working (ch 3, skip next 3 sc) where marked.

Next Row: Work sc as before, working 3 sc into each ch-3 sp of previous row.

Next Row: Work sc as before. Fasten off.

Sew on buttons.

Interlocked Triangles Jacket

Challenge your crochet skills with this roomy jacket. Featherweight mohair, worked intarsia-style throughout, produces a garment of exceptional warmth and beauty.

ADVANCED

❀ *Sizes*

Small/Medium (Large/X-Large). Instructions are for the smaller size, with changes for the larger size noted in parentheses as necessary.

❀ *Finished Measurements*

Bust (Buttoned): 50¾ (63½)"/129 (161.5) cm
Length: 32½ (34)"/82.5 (86.5) cm
Sleeve width at upper arm: 19 (22)"/48.5 (56) cm

❀ *Materials*

Berroco's *Mohair Classic* (bulky weight; 73% mohair/13% wool/9% nylon; 1½ oz/
  43 g; approx 93 yd/85 m), 10 (14) skeins Burgundy #8346 (A), 7 (10) skeins
  each of Gold #8775 (B), Loden #1107 (C), and Pumpkin #8774 (D)
Crochet hook, size J/10 (6.00 mm) or size needed to obtain gauge
Seven 1½"/38 mm buttons (One World Button Supply Company's *Burnt Horn
  Diamond Style #NPL 182* was used on sample garment)

❀ *Gauge*

In patt, 13 sts and 16 rows = 4"/10 cm.
To measure your gauge, make a test swatch as follows: Ch 14. **Foundation Row:** Sc
  into second ch from hook and into each ch across. Ch 1, turn. **Next Row:** Sc
  into each sc across. Ch 1, turn. Repeat last row 14 more times. Fasten off.
Piece should measure 4"/10 cm square. **To save time, take time to check gauge.**

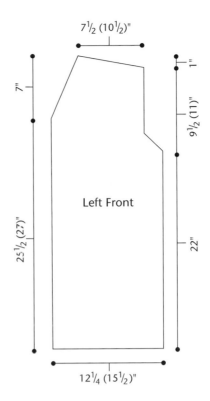

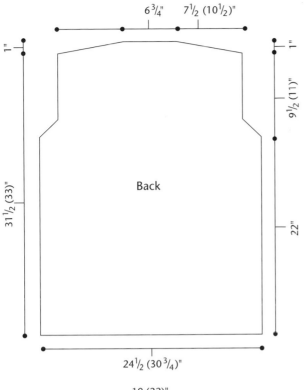

6¾" 7½ (10½)"

1" 1"

9½ (11)"

Back

31½ (33)"

22"

24½ (30¾)"

7½ (10½)"

7"

1"

9½ (11)"

Left Front

25½ (27)"

22"

12¼ (15½)"

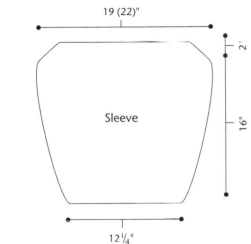

19 (22)"

2"

Sleeve

16"

12¼"

PATTERN NOTES:

- Use intarsia technique throughout. Use a separate bobbin for each section of color. Be sure to twist yarns on WS to prevent holes.
- To change color, work until 2 loops rem on hook; with second color, complete the st; fasten off first color.
- To decrease in sc, work a dec sc to combine the first 2 sts and the last 2 sts of the row.
- To increase, work 2 sts into a st.
- For a description and illustration of any unfamiliar stitch, refer to the back of the book.

❀ Back

With A, ch 81 (101).

Interlocked Diamonds Patt Row 1 (RS): Sc into second ch from hook and into next 3 ch, *change to D and work sc into next 2 ch, change to C and work sc into next 8 ch, change to B and work sc into next 2 ch, change to A and work sc into next 8 ch. Repeat from * across, ending row with change to D and work sc into next 2 ch, change to C and work sc into next 8 ch, change to B and work sc into next 2 ch, change to A and work sc into last 4 ch—80 (100) sc total. Ch 1, turn.

Cont even in Interlocked Diamonds Patt until piece measures approx 22"/56 cm from beg.

Shape Armholes: Cont in patt and work dec sc at beg and end of next row and then every other row four more times—70 (90) sts rem.

Cont even until armholes measure approx 9½ (11)"/24 (28) cm.

KEY:

■ = A

□ = B

▨ = C

▥ = D

Note:
Each square on chart represents one sc. At the end of each row, ch 1 to turn.

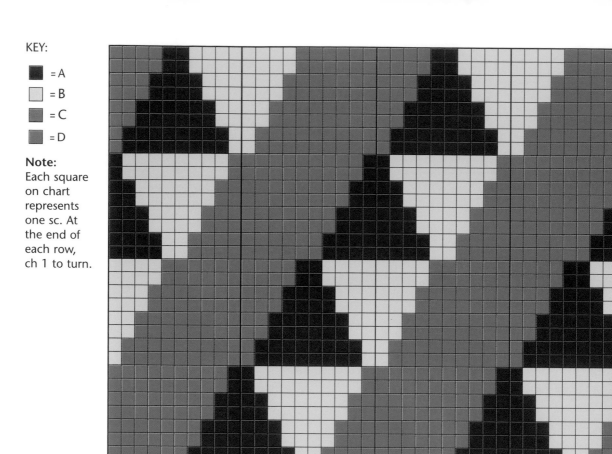

Row 32

Row 1

← 20 sc repeat →

End Back for both sizes
End Sleeves for both sizes
End Left Front for Small/Medium
End Right Front for both sizes

Beg Back for both sizes
Beg Sleeves for both sizes
Beg Left Front for both sizes
Beg Right Front for Small/Medium

End Left Front for Large/X-Large

Beg Right Front for Large/X-Large

Shape Shoulders: Slip st into first 6 (9) sts, ch 1, cont in patt across next 58 (72) sts, leave last 6 (9) sts unworked, turn.

Repeat last row two more times—34 (36) sts rem.

Next Row: Slip st into first 6 (7) sts, cont in patt across next 22 sts, leave last 6 (7) sts unworked. Fasten off.

❖ Pocket Linings (Make Two)

With A, ch 21.

Row 1 (RS): Sc into second ch from hook and into each ch across—20 sc. Ch 1, turn.

Next Row: Sc into each sc across. Ch 1, turn.

Repeat last row until piece measures approx 6"/ 15 cm from beg, ending after WS row. Fasten off.

❖ Left Front

With A, ch 41 (51).

Beg Row 1 of Interlocked Triangles Patt where indicated, and work as for back until piece mea-

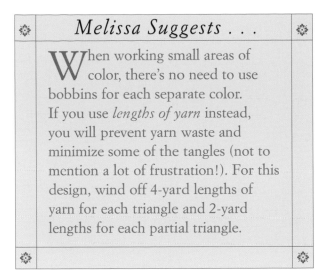

sures approx 8"/20.5 cm from beg, ending after WS row—40 (50) sc each row.

Place Pocket Lining: Next Row (RS): Cont in patt and work across first 10 (15) sts, with RS facing cont in Interlocked Triangles Patt across 20 sts of one pocket lining, skip next 20 sts of left front, work to end row.

Cont even until piece measures same as back to armholes, ending after WS row.

Shape Armhole: Cont in patt and work dec sc at beg of next row and then at armhole edge every other row four more times—35 (45) sts rem.

Cont even until piece measures approx 25½ (27)"/ 65 (68.5) cm from beg, ending after RS row.

Shape Neck: Next Row (WS): Cont in patt and work a dec sc at neck edge every row twice, then every other row nine times—24 (34) sts rem.

Cont even in patt until piece measures same as back to shoulders, ending after WS row.

Shape Shoulders: Next Row (RS): Slip st into first 6 (9) sts, ch 1, cont in patt to end row—18 (25) sts.

Next Row: Work across first 12 (16) sts, leave last 6 (9) sts unworked, turn.

Next Row: Slip st into first 6 (9) sts, ch 1, cont in patt across last 6 (7) sts. Fasten off.

❧ Right Front

Work as for left front, *except* reverse all shaping, and beg chart as indicated.

❧ Sleeves

With A, ch 41.

Skip first 8 rows of chart and beg Interlocked Diamonds Patt with Row 9; inc 1 sc each side every other row 0 (3) times, then every fourth row 4 (13) times, then every sixth row 7 (0) times—62 (72) sts.

Cont even until sleeve measures approx 16"/ 40.5 cm from beg.

Shape Cap: Cont in patt and work dec sc at beg and end of next three rows and then every other row twice—52 (62) sts rem. Fasten off.

❧ Finishing

Sew shoulder seams.

Collar and Front Bands: With RS facing and A, work 22 sc along back of neck. Cont in sc, and work into 2 additional sc on each sweater front each side every row seventeen times—90 sc.

Cont along front edge, and work 74 (80) sc to end row—164 (170) sc. Ch 1, turn.

Next Row: Sc into first 164 (170) sc, and then working along other front edge, work 74 (80) sc—238 (250) sc.

Cont even until bands measure approx ⅞"/2 cm from beg. Place markers for seven evenly spaced

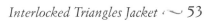

buttonholes along right front edge, making the first and last ½"/1.5 cm from neck shaping and bottom edge.

Next Row: Cont in sc, and make seven buttonholes where marked by working (ch 3, skip next 3 sc).

On next row, work 3 sc into each ch-3 sp of previous row.

Cont even until bands measure approx 1¾"/4.5 cm from beg. Fasten off.

Pocket Bands: With RS facing, attach A with a slip st to top of pocket edge and ch 1. Work 20 sc along top of pocket. Ch 1, turn.

Next Row: Sc into each sc. Repeat last row six more times. Fasten off.

Sew sides of pocket band to front. Sew pocket linings to WS of front.

Set in sleeves. Sew sleeve and side seams.

Lower Sleeve Edging: With RS facing, attach A with a slip st to sleeve seam and ch 1.

Rnd 1: Work 40 sc around lower edge of sleeve. Join with a slip st to first sc. Ch 1.

Next Rnd: Sc into each sc. Join with a slip st to first sc. Ch 1.

Repeat last row five more times. Fasten off.

Sew on buttons.

Dainty Mesh Vest

Breeze through this cropped openwork vest!
To make it even more special, add a little dash
of color with terrific buttons.

ADVANCED BEGINNER

❁ *Sizes*

Small (Medium, Large, Extra-Large). Instructions are for smallest size, with changes for other sizes noted in parentheses as necessary.

❁ *Finished Measurements*

Bust (Buttoned): 34 (38¼, 42¾, 47)"/86.5 (97, 108.5, 119.5) cm
Length (Including Edging): 18¾ (18¾, 19¾, 19¾)"/47.5 (47.5, 50, 50) cm

❁ *Materials*

Coats and Clark's *Lustersheen* (fingering weight; 100% acrylic; 1⅛ oz/51.5 g; approx 150 yd/135 m), 6 (6, 7, 8) balls Spa Blue # 821
Crochet hooks, sizes D/3 and E/4 (3.25 and 3.50 mm) or size needed to obtain gauge
Six ½"/13 mm buttons (Zecca Button Company's *Style #138A* was used on sample garment)

❁ *Gauge*

In patt with larger hook, 30 sts and 16 rows = 4"/10 cm.
To measure your gauge, make a test swatch as follows: With larger hook, ch 31. Work Mesh Patt for 16 rows. Fasten off.
Piece should measure 4"/10 cm square. **To save time, take time to check gauge.**

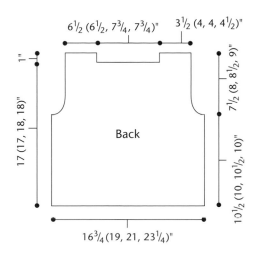

6½ (6½, 7¾, 7¾)"   3½ (4, 4, 4½)"

1"

17 (17, 18, 18)"

Back

7½ (8, 8½, 9)"

10½ (10, 10½, 10)"

16¾ (19, 21, 23¼)"

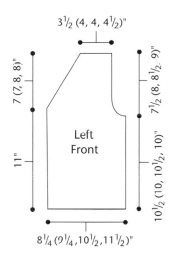

3½ (4, 4, 4½)"

7 (7, 8, 8)"

Left
Front

7½ (8, 8½, 9)"

11"

10½ (10, 10½, 10)"

8¼ (9¼, 10½, 11½)"

Note: These measurements
do not include the edging.

Pattern Notes:

- Each dc and sc counts as 1 st.
- Each turning-ch-3 counts as 1 dc.
- Each ch-2 sp counts as 2 sts.
- To decrease in dc, work until 2 sts rem in row, then work a dec dc to combine the last 2 sts in row. On the next row, work last st into the last dc, not into the top of the turning-ch-3.
- To decrease in sc, work a dec sc to combine the first 2 sts and the last 2 sts of the row.
- For a description and illustration of any unfamiliar stitch, refer to the back of the book.

Mesh Patt

Ch multiple of 4 + 3

Foundation Row 1 (WS): Sc into second ch from hook and into next ch, *ch 2, skip next 2 ch, sc into next 2 ch. Repeat from * across. Ch 3, turn.

Foundation Row 2: Skip first sc, dc into next sc, *ch 2, skip next 2 ch, dc into next 2 sc. Repeat from * across. Ch 1, turn.

Row 1 (WS): Sc into first 2 dc, *ch 2, sc into next 2 dc. Repeat from * across, ending row with ch 2, sc into next dc, sc into top of turning-ch-3. Ch 3, turn.

Row 2: Skip first sc, dc into next sc, *ch 2, dc into next 2 sc. Repeat from * across. Ch 1, turn.

Repeat Rows 1 and 2 for patt.

Back

With larger hook, ch 127 (143, 159, 175). Beg Mesh Patt, and work even on 126 (142, 158, 174) sts until piece measures approx 10½ (10, 10½, 10)"/26.5 (25.5, 26.5, 25.5) cm from beg, ending after WS row. Fasten off.

Shape Armholes: Next Row (RS): With RS facing and larger hook, skip the first 12 (16, 20, 24) sts, attach yarn with a slip st to next sc and ch 3. Work patt as established across next 102 (110, 118, 126) sts. Ch 1, turn, leaving rest of row unworked.

Cont even in patt until armholes measure approx 6½ (7, 7½, 8)"/16.5 (18, 19, 20.5) cm, ending after WS row.

Shape Neck: Next Row (RS): Work patt across first 26 (30, 30, 34) sts, ch 1, turn, leaving rest of row unworked.

Cont even on this side until armhole measures approx 7½ (8, 8½, 9)"/19 (20.5, 21.5, 23) cm, ending after WS row. Fasten off.

For second side of neck shaping, with RS facing, skip the middle 50 (50, 58, 58) sts and attach yarn with a slip st to next st and ch 3, work patt across to end row—26 (30, 30, 34) sts.

Complete as for first side.

❀ Right Front

With larger hook, ch 63 (71, 79, 87). Beg Mesh Patt, and work even on 62 (70, 78, 86) sts until piece measures approx 10½ (10, 10½, 10)"/26.5 (25.5, 26.5, 25.5) cm from beg, ending after WS row.

Shape Armhole: Next Row (RS): Work patt as established across first 50 (54, 58, 62) sts, ch 1, turn, leaving last 12 (16, 20, 24) sts unworked.

Cont even in patt until armhole measures approx ½ (1, ½, 1)"/1.5 (2.5, 1.5, 2.5) cm, ending after WS row. Ch 1, turn.

Shape Neck: Dec Row 1 (RS): Skip first sc, sc into next sc, *ch 2, dc into next 2 sc. Repeat from * across, ch 1, turn.

Dec Row 2: Work patt as established across until 4 sts rem in row, ending row with dec sc to combine next dc and ch-2 sp. Ch 1, turn.

Next Two Rows: Work even in patt as established. Repeat last four rows 5 (5, 6, 6) more times—26 (30, 30, 34) sts rem.

Cont even until piece measures same as back. Fasten off.

❀ Left Front

Work as for right front until piece measures approx 10½ (10, 10½, 10)"/26.5 (25.5, 26.5, 25.5) cm from beg, ending after RS row. Fasten off.

Shape Armhole: With WS facing and larger hook, skip first 12 (16, 20, 24) sts, and attach yarn with a slip st to next st and ch 1. Work patt as established across 50 (54, 58, 62) sts to end row.

Cont even in patt until armhole measures approx ½ (1, ½, 1)"/1.5 (2.5, 1.5, 2.5) cm, ending after WS row.

Shape Neck: Dec Row 1 (RS): Work patt as established across row until 2 sts rem, ending row with dec sc to combine next 2 sc. Ch 1, turn.

Dec Row 2: Dec sc to combine first ch-2 sp and next dc, sc into next dc, cont in patt across to end row.

Next Two Rows: Work even in patt as established. Repeat last four rows 5 (5, 6, 6) more times—26 (30, 30, 34) sts rem.

Complete as for right front.

❀ Finishing

Lower Back Edging: Row 1 (RS): With RS facing and smaller hook, attach yarn with a slip st to first ch of foundation ch and ch 1.

Row 1 (RS): Working into unworked loops of foundation ch, work sc into first 2 ch, *sc into next ch, skip next ch, sc into next 2 ch. Repeat from * across. Ch 1, turn.

Rows 2–4: Sc into each sc across, ch 1, turn. After Row 4, ch 3 to turn.

Row 5: Skip first 2 sc, *into next sc work (2 dc, ch 3, slip st into last dc just made, dc), skip next 2 sc. Repeat from * across, ending row with (2 dc, ch 3, slip st into last dc just made, dc) into next sc, skip next sc, dc into last sc. Fasten off.

Lower Front Edgings: Work same as lower back edging

Sew shoulder seams.

Sew side seams.

Front Bands: With RS facing and smaller hook, attach yarn to lower right front edge and ch 1. Work one row sc up right front, around neck, and down left front.

Next Row: Work sc into each sc, working 2 sc at beg of front neck shaping and 1 dec sc at beg of each side of back neck shaping.

Place markers for six evenly spaced buttonholes along left front, making the first ½"/1.5 cm from bottom edge and the last ¼"/0.5 cm from beg of neck shaping.

Next Row: Work sc as before, making six 3-st buttonholes by working (ch 3, skip next 3 sc) where marked.

Next Row: Work sc as before, working 3 sc into each ch-3 sp from previous row. Ch 3, turn.

Next Row: Skip first 2 sc, *(2 dc, ch 3, slip st into last dc just made, dc) into next sc, skip next 2 sc. Repeat from * across, ending row with (2 dc, ch 3, slip st into last dc just made, dc) into next sc, skip next sc, dc into last sc. *Note:* Adjust sts as necessary to end row evenly in patt. Fasten off.

Armhole Bands: With RS facing and smaller hook, attach yarn to underarm with a slip st and ch 1. Work three rnds sc around armhole, working a dec sc at shoulder seam and at top of side seam each rnd. Fasten off.

Sew on buttons.

Chenille A-Line Tunic

Bring style to the holiday season with this swing tunic and its flared sleeves. Here, solid and lacy fabrics meet in a romantic empire waist design.

INTERMEDIATE

❀ *Sizes*

Small (Medium, Large, Extra-Large). Instructions are for smallest size, with changes for other sizes noted in parentheses as necessary.

❀ *Finished Measurements*

Bust: 34 (37, 40, 43)"/86.5 (94, 101.5, 109) cm
Length: 28 (29, 30, 31)"/71 (73.5, 76, 78.5) cm

❀ *Materials*

Lion Brand's *Chenille Sensations* (heavy worsted weight; 100% Acrilan® acrylic;
   1⅜ oz/40 g; approx 87 yd/80 m), 18 (20, 22, 24) skeins Purple #147
Crochet hook, size H/8 (5.00 mm) or size needed to obtain gauge

❀ *Gauge*

In solid sc, 16 sts and 18 rows = 4"/10 cm.
To measure your gauge, make a test swatch as follows: Ch 17. **Foundation Row:** Sc
   into second ch from hook and into each ch across. Ch 1, turn. **Next Row:** Sc
   into each sc across. Ch 1, turn. Repeat last row 16 more times. Fasten off.
Piece should measure 4"/10 cm square. **To save time, take time to check gauge.**

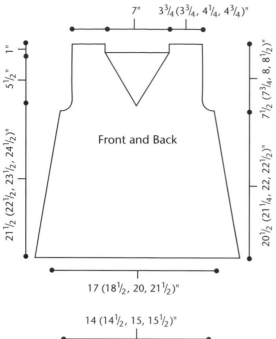

7" 3¾ (3¾, 4¼, 4¾)"

1"

5½"

7½ (7¾, 8, 8½)"

Front and Back

21½ (22½, 23½, 24½)"

20½ (21¼, 22, 22½)"

17 (18½, 20, 21½)"

14 (14½, 15, 15½)"

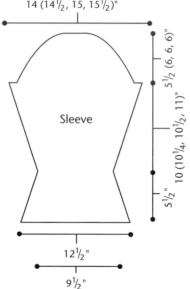

5½ (6, 6, 6)"

Sleeve

10 (10¼, 10½, 11)"

5½"

12½"

9½"

Pattern Note:

- For a description and illustration of any unfamiliar stitch, refer to the back of the book.

❀ Back

Ch 113 (123, 133, 143).

Foundation Row (RS): Dc into fourth ch from hook and into next 3 ch, *ch 1, skip next ch, dc

into next 4 ch. Repeat from * across, ending row with ch 1, skip next ch, dc into last 5 ch. Ch 1, turn.

Next Row: Sc into first dc, *ch 4, sc into next ch-1 sp. Repeat from * across, ending row with ch 4, sc into top of turning-ch-3. Ch 3, turn.

Next Row (RS): Skip first sc, *4 dc into next ch-4 sp, ch 1, skip next sc. Repeat from * across, ending row with 4 dc into next ch-4 sp, dc into last sc. Ch 1, turn.

Repeat last two rows until piece measures approx 8½"/21.5 cm from beg, ending after RS row. Ch 1, turn.

Next Row (WS): Sc into first dc, *ch 4, sc into next ch-1 sp, ch 3 (instead of ch 4), sc into next ch-1 sp. Repeat from * across, ending row with ch 4, sc into top of turning-ch-3. Ch 3, turn.

Next Row: Skip first sc, *3 dc into next ch-3 sp, ch 1, skip next sc, 4 dc into next ch-4 sp, ch 1, skip next sc. Repeat from * across, ending row with 4 dc into next ch-4 sp, dc into last dc. Ch 1, turn.

Repeat last two rows until piece measures approx 16½ (17, 17¼, 17½)"/42 (43, 44, 44.5) cm from beg, ending after WS row. Ch 1, turn.

Next Row (RS): Sc into first sc, *3 sc into next ch-sp, skip next sc. Repeat from * across, ending row with 3 sc into next ch-sp, sc into last sc. Ch 1, turn—68 (74, 80, 86) sc.

Cont even in sc until piece measures approx 20½ (21¼, 22, 22½)"/52 (54, 56, 57) cm from beg, ending after WS row. *Do not ch 1 to turn.*

Shape Armholes: Next Row (RS): Slip st into first 2 (3, 4, 5) sts, ch 1, sc into next 64 (68, 72, 76) sc, ch 1, turn, leaving rest of row unworked.

Cont in sc and work a dec sc each side every row 2 (3, 3, 3) times, then every other row 1 (2, 2, 2) times—58 (58, 62, 66) sc rem.

Cont even until armholes measure approx 6½ (6¾, 7, 7½)"/16.5 (17, 18, 19) cm, ending after WS row. Ch 1, turn.

Shape Neck: Next Row (RS): Sc into first 15 (15, 17, 19) sc, ch 1, turn, leaving rest of row unworked.

Cont in sc on these 15 (15, 17, 19) shoulder sts until armholes measure approx 7½ (7¾, 8, 8½)"/19 (19.5, 20.5, 21.5) cm. Fasten off.

For second side of neck shaping, with RS facing, skip the middle 28 sc and attach yarn with a slip st to next sc and work 15 (15, 17, 19) sc to end row. Complete as for first side.

❀ Front

Work as for back until 4 (6, 6, 8) rows of armhole shaping are completed—60 (60, 64, 66) sts rem. Ch 1, turn.

Shape Neck: Next Row (RS): Cont armhole shaping as for back, **and at the same time,** work across row until 30 (30, 32, 33) sts rem in row. Ch 1, turn, leaving rest of row unworked.

❀ Melissa Suggests . . .

Would you enjoy a spring or summer version of this pretty yet practical sweater? Try substituting cotton yarn for the chenille. For a proper fit, make sure that the stitch gauges match.

Work a dec sc at neck edge every row four times, then every other row ten times—15 (15, 17, 19) sc rem.

Cont even until armhole measures same as back. Fasten off.

For second side of neck, with RS facing, attach yarn with a slip st to next sc and ch 1. Complete as for first side.

❀ Sleeves

Ch 63.

Foundation Row (RS): Dc into fourth ch from hook and into next 3 ch, *ch 1, skip next ch, dc into next 4 ch. Repeat from * across, ending row with ch 1, skip next ch, dc into last 5 ch. Ch 1, turn.

Next Row: Sc into first dc, *ch 4, sc into next ch-1 sp. Repeat from * across, ending row with ch 4, sc into top of turning-ch-3. Ch 3, turn.

Next Row: Skip first sc, *4 dc into next ch-4 sp, ch 1, skip next sc. Repeat from * across, ending row with 4 dc into next ch-4 sp, dc into last sc. Ch 1, turn.

Repeat last two rows until piece measures approx 3½"/9 cm from beg, ending after RS row. Ch 1, turn.

Next Row (WS): Sc into first dc, *ch 3, sc into next ch 1 sp. Repeat from * across, ending row with ch 3, sc into top of turning-ch-3. Ch 3, turn.

Next Row: Skip first sc, *3 dc into next ch-3 sp, ch 1, skip next sc. Repeat from * across, ending row with 3 dc into next ch-3 sp, dc into last dc. Ch 1, turn.

Repeat last two rows until piece measures approx 5½"/14 cm from beg, ending after WS row. Ch 1, turn.

Next Row (RS): Sc into first sc, *3 sc into next ch-3 sp, skip next sc. Repeat from * across, ending row with 3 sc into next ch-3 sp, sc into last sc. Ch 1, turn—38 sc.

Cont in sc, and inc 1 sc each side every fourth row 7 (9, 11, 12) times, then every sixth row 2 (1, 0, 0) times—56 (58, 60, 62) sc.

Work even until sleeve measures approx 15½ (15¾, 16, 16½)"/39.5 (40, 40.5, 42) cm from beg, ending after WS row. *Do not ch 1 to turn.*

Shape Cap: Next Row (RS): Slip st into first 2 (3, 4, 5) sc, ch 1, sc into next 52 sc, ch 1, turn, leaving rest of row unworked.

Work a dec sc each side every other row twice, then every row twenty times—8 sc rem. Fasten off.

✿ Finishing

Sew shoulder seams.

Neckband: With RS facing, attach yarn with a slip st at neck edge of right shoulder seam and ch 1.

Rnd 1: Work 36 sc evenly along back of neckline, 28 sc along right side of front neck shaping, 28 sc along left side of front neck shaping, join with a slip st to first sc. Ch 1.

Rnd 2: Sc into each sc, working dec sc at center front and at beg of each side of back neck shaping. Fasten off.

Set in sleeves. Sew sleeve and side seams.

Bottom Border: With RS facing, attach yarn with a slip st to lower right side seam and ch 1.

Rnd 1: Working along opposite side of foundation ch, work 220 (240, 260, 280) sc around lower edge. Join with slip st to first sc. Ch 1.

Rnd 2: Sc into each sc, ending rnd with a slip st to first sc. Fasten off.

Sleeve Border: With RS facing, attach yarn with a slip st to lower sleeve seam and ch 1.

Rnd 1: Working along opposite side of foundation ch, work 60 sc around lower edge. Join with a slip st to first sc. Ch 1.

Rnd 2: Sc into each sc, ending rnd with a slip st to first sc. Fasten off.

Breezy Summertime Cardigan

Toss this piece over your favorite jeans and head out the door! An ombré yarn worked in a shell pattern stitch creates the pretty watercolor effect.

INTERMEDIATE

❁ Sizes

Small (Medium, Large, Extra-Large). Instructions are for smallest size, with changes for other sizes noted in parentheses as necessary.

❁ Finished Measurements

Bust (Buttoned): 36¾ (41½, 46½, 51½)"/93.5 (105.5, 118, 131) cm
Length (Including Border): 26¾ (26¾, 29½, 29½)"/68 (68, 75, 75) cm
Sleeve width at upper arm: 18 (18, 20½, 20½)"/45.5 (45.5, 52, 52) cm

❁ Materials

Lily's *Sugar 'n' Cream Sport* (sport weight; 100% cotton; 1¾ oz/50 g and approx
   108 yd/100 m for solid colors; 1½ oz/42.5 g and 108 yd/98 m for variegated colors),
   8 (8, 9, 10) skeins White #01 (A) and 12 (12, 13, 13) skeins Mountain Stream
   #105 (B)
Crochet hook, size F/5 (3.75 mm) or size needed to obtain gauge
Seven ⅞"/22 mm buttons (One World Button Supply Company's *Glass Triangle
   Button Style #GHB 131LBL* was used on sample garment)

❁ Gauge

In patt, 20 sts and 11 rows = 4"/10 cm.
To measure your gauge, make a test swatch as follows: Ch 26. Work even in Two-
   Color Shell Patt on 25 sts for 12 rows. Fasten off.
Piece should measure 5"/13 cm wide and 4"/10 cm long. **To save time, take time to
   check gauge.**

ERICAN PORCUPINE

rodents live on a diet
k and other vegetation.
resting in trees and
r home in rocky dens
heir protective quills
ith sharp barbs and
but cannot be shot

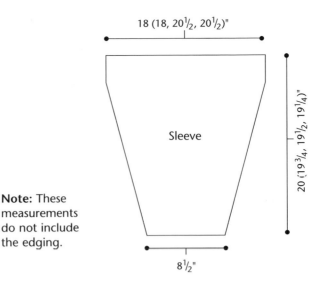

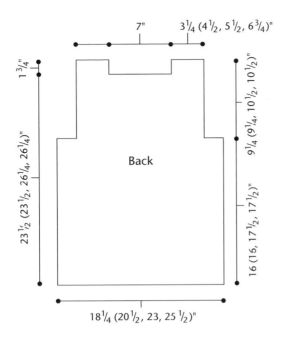

7" 3¼ (4½, 5½, 6¾)"

1¾"

Back

9¼ (9¼, 10½, 10½)"

23½ (23½, 26¼, 26¼)"

16 (16, 17½, 17½)"

18¼ (20½, 23, 25½)"

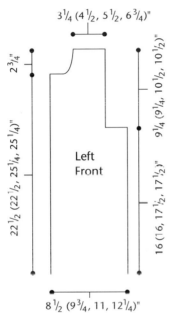

3¼ (4½, 5½, 6¾)"

2¾"

Left
Front

9¼ (9¼, 10½, 10½)"

22½ (22½, 25¼, 25¼)"

16 (16, 17½, 17½)"

8½ (9¾, 11, 12¼)"

18 (18, 20½, 20½)"

Sleeve

20 (19¾, 19½, 19¼)"

8½"

Note: These measurements do not include the edging.

❧ *Two-Color Shell Patt*

Ch multiple of 6 + 2

Foundation Row (WS): With A, sc into second ch from hook, *ch 2, skip next 2 ch, dc into next ch, ch 2, skip next 2 ch, sc into next ch. Repeat from * across. Change to B, ch 3, turn.

Row 1 (RS): With B, 2 dc into first sc, *sc into next dc, 5 dc into next sc. Repeat from * across, ending row with sc into next dc, 3 dc into last sc. Change to A, ch 1, turn.

Row 2: With A, sc into first dc, *ch 2, skip next 2 dc, BPDC into next dc two rows below, ch 2, skip next 2 dc, sc into next dc. Repeat from * across, ending row with ch 2, skip next 2 dc, BPDC into next dc two rows below, ch 2, sc into top of turning-ch-3. Ch 3, turn.

Row 3: Skip first sc; with A, *2 dc into next ch-2 sp, dc into next st. Repeat from * across. Ch 1, turn.

Row 4: With A, sc into first dc, *ch 2, skip next 2 dc, dc into next dc, ch 2, skip next 2 dc, sc into next dc. Repeat from * across, ending row with ch 2, skip next 2 dc, dc into next dc, ch 2, skip next 2 dc, sc into top of turning-ch-3. Change to B, ch 3, turn.

Repeat Rows 1–4 for patt.

PATTERN NOTES:

- Unless noted otherwise, always skip the st behind the BPDC.
- Each turning-ch-3 counts as 1 dc.
- To change color, work until 2 loops rem on hook; with second color, complete the st; fasten off first color.
- For a description and illustration of any unfamiliar stitch, refer to the back of the book.

❧ Back

With A, ch 92 (104, 116, 128). Beg Two-Color Shell Patt, and work even on 91 (103, 115, 127) sts until piece measures approx 16 (16, 17½, 17½)"/ 40.5 (40.5, 44.5, 44.5) cm from beg, ending after Row 3 of patt. *Do not ch 1 to turn.*

Shape Armholes: Next Row (WS): Slip st into first 13 sts, ch 1, sc into same dc as slip st, cont in patt as established across next 66 (78, 90, 102) sts, turn, leaving last 12 sts of row unworked.

Cont even in patt on 67 (79, 91, 103) sts until armholes measure approx 7½ (7½, 8¾, 8¾)"/19 (19, 22, 22) cm, ending after Row 2 of patt.

Shape Neck: Next Row (RS): Cont in patt as established across first 16 (22, 28, 34) dc, ch 5, turn.

Next Row: Skip first 3 dc, *sc into next dc, ch 2, skip next 2 dc, dc into next dc. Repeat from * across, ending row with sc into top of turning-ch-3. Change to B, ch 3, turn.

Next Row: 2 dc into first sc, *sc into next dc, 5 dc into next sc. Repeat from * across, ending row with sc into third ch of turning-ch-5. Change to A, ch 5, turn.

Next Row: Skip first sc and next 2 dc, *sc into next dc, ch 2, skip next 2 dc, BPDC into next dc two rows below, ch 2, skip next 2 dc. Repeat from * across, ending row with sc into top of turning-ch-3. Ch 3, turn.

Next Row: Skip first st, *2 dc into next ch-2 sp, dc into next st. Repeat from * across. Fasten off.

For second side of neck, with RS facing, skip the middle 12 ch-2 spaces, attach color A with a slip st to next st and ch 3.

Next Row (RS): *2 dc into next ch-2 sp, dc into next st. Repeat from * across. Ch 1, turn.

Next Row: Sc into first dc, *ch 2, skip next 2 dc, sc into next dc, ch 2, skip next 2 dc, dc into next dc. Repeat from * across, ending row with ch 2, dc into top of turning-ch-3. Change to B, ch 1, turn.

Next Row: Sc into first st, *5 dc into next sc, sc into next dc. Repeat from * across, ending row with 3 dc into last sc. Change to A, ch 1, turn.

Next Row: Sc into first st, *ch 2, skip next 2 dc, BPDC into next dc two rows below, ch 2, skip next 2 dc, sc into next dc. Repeat from * across, ending row with ch 2, skip next 2 dc, dc into last sc. Ch 3, turn.

Next Row: Skip first st, *2 dc into next ch-2 sp, dc into next st. Repeat from * across. Fasten off.

❧ Left Front

With A, ch 44 (50, 56, 62). Beg Two-Color Shell Patt, and work even on 43 (49, 55, 61) sts until piece measures approx 16 (16, 17½, 17½)"/ 40.5 (40.5, 44.5, 44.5) cm from beg, ending after Row 3 of patt. Ch 1, turn.

Shape Armhole: Next Row (WS): Work in patt across until 12 sts rem in row. Ch 1, turn, leaving last 12 sts of row unworked.

Cont even in patt on 31 (37, 43, 49) sts until armhole measures approx 6¼ (6¼, 7½, 7½)"/16 (16, 19, 19) cm, ending after Row 3 of patt. *Do not ch 1 to turn.*

Shape Neck: Next Row (WS): With A, slip st into first 4 dc, ch 5, skip next 2 dc, *sc into next dc, ch 2, skip next 2 dc, dc into next dc, ch 2, skip next 2 dc. Repeat from * across, ending row with sc into top of turning-ch-3. Change to B, ch 3, turn.

Next Row: 2 dc into first sc, *sc into next dc, 5 dc into next sc. Repeat from * 3 (4, 5, 6) more times,

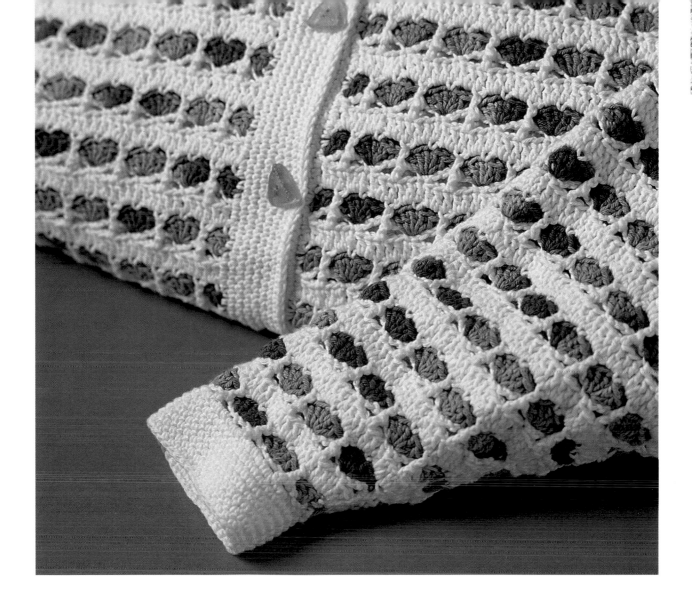

then skip next 2 dc, sc into third ch of turning-ch-5. Fasten off B.

Next Row: With WS facing, skip the last sc and the first 2 dc of last row, and attach A with a slip st to next dc and ch 1. Sc into same dc as slip st, *ch 2, skip next 2 dc, BPDC into next dc two rows below, ch 2, skip next 2 dc, sc into next dc. Repeat from * across, ending row with ch 2, skip next 2 dc, BPDC into next dc two rows below, ch 2, skip next 2 dc, sc into top of turning-ch-3. Ch 3, turn.

Next Row: Skip first st, *2 dc into next ch-2 sp, dc into next st. Repeat from * across, ending row with 2 dc into next ch-2 sp, yarn over, insert hook into next st and pull up a loop, yarn over and draw it through 2 loops, (yarn over, insert hook into ch-2 sp and pull up a loop, yarn over and draw it through 2 loops) twice, yarn over, insert hook into last st and pull up a loop, yarn over and draw it through 2 loops, yarn over and draw it through all 5 loops on hook. Ch 5, turn.

Next Row: Skip first dec-st and next 2 dc, *sc into next dc, ch 2, skip next 2 dc, dc into next dc, ch 2, skip next 2 dc. Repeat from * across, ending row with sc into top of turning-ch-3. Change to B, ch 3, turn.

Next Row: 2 dc into first sc, *sc into next dc, 5 dc into next sc. Repeat from * across, ending row with sc into third ch of turning-ch-5. Fasten off B.

Next Row: With WS facing, skip the last sc and the first 2 dc of last row; attach A with a slip st to next dc and ch 1. Sc into same dc as slip st, *ch 2, skip next 2 dc, BPDC into next dc two rows below, ch 2, skip next 2 dc, sc into next dc. Repeat from * across, ending row with ch 2, skip next 2 dc, BPDC into next dc two rows below, ch 2, skip next 2 dc, sc into top of turning-ch-3. Ch 3, turn.

Next Row: Skip first st, *2 dc into next ch-2 sp, dc into next st. Repeat from * across. Fasten off.

❀ Right Front

Work same as left front until piece measures approx 16 (16, 17½, 17½)"/40.5 (40.5, 44.5, 44.5) cm from beg, ending after Row 3 of patt. *Do not ch 1 to turn.*

Shape Armhole: Next Row (WS): With A, slip st into the first 13 sts, ch 1, sc into same dc as slip st, work to end row.

Cont even in patt on 31 (37, 43, 49) sts as established until armhole measures approx 6¼ (6¼, 7½, 7½)"/16 (16, 19, 19) cm, ending after Row 3 of patt. Ch 1, turn.

Shape Neck: Next Row (WS): Work in patt until 3 sts rem. Change to B, ch 1, turn, leaving last 3 sts unworked.

Next Row: Sc into first dc, *5 dc into next sc, sc into next dc. Repeat from * across, ending row with 3 dc into last sc. Change to A, ch 1, turn.

Next Row: Sc into first dc, *ch 2, skip next 2 dc, BPDC into next dc two rows below, ch 2, skip next 2 dc, sc into next dc. Repeat from * across, leaving last 2 dc and sc unworked. Ch 3, turn.

Next Row: (Yarn over, insert hook into next ch-2 sp and pull up a loop, yarn over and draw it through 2 loops on hook) twice, yarn over, insert

hook into next st and pull up a loop, yarn over and draw it through 2 loops on hook, yarn over and draw it through all 4 loops on hook, *2 dc into next ch-2 sp, dc into next st. Repeat from * across. Ch 1, turn.

Next Row: Sc into first dc, *ch 2, skip next 2 dc, dc into next dc, ch 2, skip next 2 dc, sc into next dc. Repeat from * across, ending row with ch 2, skip next 2 dc, dc into dec-st. Change to B, ch 1, turn.

Next Row: 5 dc into first sc, *sc into next dc, 5 dc into next sc. Repeat from * across, ending row with sc into next dc, 3 dc into last sc. Change to A, ch 1, turn.

Next Row: Sc into first dc, *ch 2, skip next 2 dc, BPDC into next dc two rows below, ch 2, skip next 2 dc, sc into next dc. Repeat from * across, ending row with ch 2, skip next 2 dc, BPDC into next dc two rows below, skip next 2 dc, dc into next dc. Ch 3, turn.

Next Row: 2 dc into first ch-2 sp, *dc into next st, 2 dc into next ch-2 sp. Repeat from * across, ending row with dc into last st. Fasten off.

❧ Sleeves

With A, ch 44. Work 3 rows of Two-Color Shell Patt on 43 sts. Ch 3, turn.

Sleeve Inc Row (RS): 3 dc into the same dc as turning-ch, *2 dc into next ch-2 sp, dc into next st. Repeat from * across, ending row with 2 dc into next ch-2 sp, 4 dc into top of turning-ch-3. Ch 5, turn.

Next Row: Skip first 3 dc, *sc into next dc, ch 2, skip next 2 dc, dc into next dc, ch 2, skip next 2 dc. Repeat from * across, ending row with sc into next dc, ch 2, skip next 2 dc, dc into top of turning-ch-3. Change to B, ch 1, turn.

Next Row: Sc into first dc, *5 dc into next sc, sc into next dc. Repeat from * across, ending row with 5 dc into next sc, sc into third ch of turning-ch-5. Change to A, ch 1, turn.

Next Row: BPDC into first dc two rows below, *ch 2, skip next 2 dc, sc into next dc, ch 2, skip next 2 dc, BPDC into next dc two rows below. Repeat from * across, ending row with ch 2, skip next 2 dc, sc into next dc, ch 2, BPDC around turning-ch-3 two rows below. Ch 3, turn.

Next Row: Work same as Sleeve Inc Row.

Next Row: Work same as Row 4 of Two-Color Shell Patt.

Next Two Rows: Work same as Rows 1 and 2 of Two-Color Shell Patt.

Repeat last 8 rows three more times, then work first four rows 0 (0, 1, 1) more time.

Cont even until sleeve measures approx 20 (19¾, 19½, 19¼)"/51 (50, 49.5, 49) cm from beg. Fasten off.

❧ Finishing

Sew shoulder seams.

Set in sleeves. Sew sleeve and side seams.

Front Bands and Lower Edging: With RS facing, attach A with a slip st to lower right side seam and ch 1. Work sc evenly along bottom of right front, up center front, around back of neck, down left front, and around lower back, working 3 sc into corners, to prevent curling, and a dec sc at each side of back neck. Join with slip st to first sc. Ch 1.

Cont in sc, increasing and decreasing in this way until band measures approx ¾"/2 cm. Place markers for seven evenly spaced buttonholes along right front, making the first and last ½"/1.5 cm from beg of neck shaping and bottom edge.

Next Rnd: Cont in sc, increasing and decreasing as before, and work seven buttonholes where marked by working (ch 4, skip next 4 sc).

Next Rnd: Cont in sc, increasing and decreasing as before, and work 4 sc into each ch-4 sp from previous rnd.

Cont in sc, increasing and decreasing as before, until band measures approx 1½"/4 cm. Fasten off.

Sleeve Edges: With RS facing, attach A with a slip st to seam and ch 1. Work rnds of sc for approx 1½"/4 cm. Fasten off.

Sew on buttons.

Waffle Stitch Pullover

Here's an ideal sweater for blustery winter days. The textured stitch pattern holds in warmth, while the ribbed neckline zips up high to keep out chills.

INTERMEDIATE

❀ *Sizes*

Small (Medium, Large, Extra-Large). Instructions are for smallest size, with changes for other sizes noted in parentheses as necessary.

❀ *Finished Measurements*

Bust: 41 (45, 48½, 52)"/104 (114.5, 123, 132) cm
Length: 27 (28, 29, 30)"/68.5 (71, 73.5, 76) cm
Sleeve width at underarm: 17 (18, 19, 20¼)"/43 (45.5, 48.5, 51.5) cm

❀ *Materials*

Plymouth's *Encore* (worsted weight; 75% acrylic/25% wool; 3½ oz/100 g; approx
   200 yd/182 m), 14 (15, 16, 16) skeins Teal #213
Crochet hooks, sizes G/6 and H/8 (4.25 and 5.00 mm) or size needed to obtain
   gauge
9"/23 cm sport zipper

❀ *Gauge*

In patt, with larger hook, 18 sts and 10 rows = 4"/10 cm.
To measure your gauge, make a test swatch as follows: With larger hook, ch 19.
   Foundation Row (RS): Dc into fourth ch from hook and into each ch across.
   Ch 3, turn. Cont in Waffle St Patt for nine more rows. Fasten off.
Piece should measure 3¾"/9.5 cm wide and 4"/10 cm long. **To save time, take time
   to check gauge.**

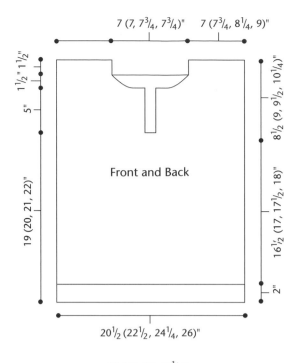

7 (7, 7¾, 7¾)"   7 (7¾, 8¼, 9)"

1½ 1½"

5"

8½ (9, 9½, 10¼)"

Front and Back

19 (20, 21, 22)"

16½ (17, 17½, 18)"

2"

20½ (22½, 24¼, 26)"

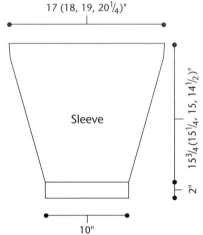

17 (18, 19, 20¼)"

Sleeve

15¾ (15¼, 15, 14½)"

2"

10"

Pattern Notes:

- Unless noted otherwise, always skip the st behind the BPDC.
- Each turning-ch-2 counts as 1 hdc.
- Each turning-ch-3 counts as 1 dc.
- To decrease in dc, work until 2 sts rem in row, then work a dec dc to combine the last 2 sts in row. On the next row, work last st into the last dc, not into the top of the turning-ch-3.
- To increase, work 2 sts into a st.
- For a description and illustration of any un-familiar stitch, refer to the back of the book.

❁ Rib Patt

Ch multiple of 2 + 1

Foundation Row (RS): Dc into fourth ch from hook and into each ch across. Ch 2, turn.

Row 1 (WS): Skip first st, *FPDC into next st, BPDC into next st. Repeat from * across, ending row with FPDC into next st, hdc into top of turning-ch-2. Ch 2, turn.

Row 2: Skip first st, *BPDC into next st, FPDC into next st. Repeat from * across, ending row with BPDC into next st, hdc into top of turning-ch-2. Ch 2, turn.

Repeat Rows 1 and 2 for patt.

❁ Waffle St Patt

Row 1 (WS): Skip first st, *FPDC into next 3 dc, dc into next dc. Repeat from * across, ending row with FPDC into next 3 dc, dc into top of turning-ch. Ch 3, turn.

Row 2: Skip first st, *dc into next 3 sts, FPDC into next st. Repeat from * across, ending row with dc into next 3 sts, dc into top of turning-ch-3. Ch 3, turn.

Repeat Rows 1 and 2 for patt.

❁ Back

With larger hook, ch 95 (103, 111, 119). Work Rib Patt on 93 (101, 109, 117) sts until piece measures approx 2"/5 cm from beg, ending after RS row.

Beg Waffle St Patt, and work even until piece measures approx 25½ (26½, 27½, 28½)"/65 (67.5, 70, 72.5) cm from beg, ending after RS row. Ch 3, turn.

Shape Neck: Next Row (WS): Skip first st, cont in patt across next 30 (34, 36, 40) sts, ch 2, turn, leaving rest of row unworked.

Work even until this side measures approx 27 (28, 29, 30)"/68.5 (71, 73.5, 76) cm from beg. Fasten off.

For second side of neck, with WS facing, skip the middle 31 (31, 35, 35) sts, and attach yarn with a slip st to next sc and ch 3. Complete as for first side.

❀ Front

Work as for back until piece measures approx 19 (20, 21, 22)"/48.5 (51, 53.5, 56) cm from beg, ending after RS row. Ch 3, turn.

Divide for Zipper Opening: Next Row (WS): Skip first st, cont in patt across next 44 (48, 52, 56) sts, ch 3, turn, leaving rest of row unworked.

Cont even until this side measures approx 24 (25, 26, 27)"/61 (63.5, 66, 68.5) cm from beg, ending after WS row. *Do not ch 3 to turn.*

Shape First Side of Neck: Next Row (RS): Slip st into first 9 (9, 11, 11) sts, ch 3, skip next st, cont in patt to end row.

Dec 1 st at neck edge every row six times—31 (35, 37, 41) sts rem.

Cont even until piece measures same as back to shoulder. Fasten off.

Second Side of Zipper Opening: With WS facing, skip the middle 3 sts and attach yarn with a slip st to next st and ch 3. Cont in patt as established to end row.

Cont even until this side measures approx 24 (25, 26, 27)"/61 (63.5, 66, 68.5) cm from beg, ending after WS row. *Do not ch 3 to turn.*

Shape Second Side of Neck: Next Row (RS): Work in patt across first 37 (41, 43, 47) sts, ch 3, turn.

Complete as for first side.

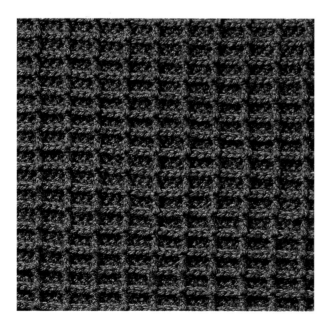

❋ Sleeves

With larger hook, ch 47. Work Rib Patt on 45 sts until piece measures approx 2"/5 cm from beg, ending after RS row.

Beg Waffle St Patt, and inc 1 st each side every row 0 (2, 8, 14) times, then every other row 16 (16, 12, 9) times—77 (81, 85, 91) sts.

Work even until sleeve measures approx 17¾ (17¼, 17, 16½)"/45 (44, 43, 42) cm from beg, ending after RS row. Fasten off.

❋ Finishing

Sew shoulder seams.

Neckband: With RS facing and smaller hook, attach yarn with a slip st to beg of neck shaping on right front and ch 3. Work 113 (113, 119, 119) dc along neck edge, working a dec dc at each of the four inside corners of front and back neck shaping. Ch 2, turn.

Repeat Rows 1 and 2 of Rib Patt until neckband measures approx 4"/10 cm from beg. Fasten off.

Zipper Facing: With RS facing and smaller hook, attach yarn with a slip st to top LH side of zipper opening and ch 1. Work one row of sc around zipper opening, working a dec sc at each lower corner of opening.

Sew in zipper.

Place markers 8½ (9, 9½, 10¼)"/21.5 (23, 24, 26) cm down from shoulders. Set in sleeves between markers. Sew sleeve and side seams.

Melinda's Textured Short-Sleeved Cardigan

Two great textured stitch patterns result in this modern basic. It is as enjoyable to make as it is to wear!

INTERMEDIATE

❀ *Sizes*

Small (Medium, Large, Extra-Large). Instructions are for smallest size, with changes for other sizes noted in parentheses as necessary.

❀ *Finished Measurements*

Bust (Buttoned): 40 (43, 46, 49)"/101.5 (109, 116.5, 124.5) cm
Length (Including Edging): 21 (22, 22½, 23)"/53.5 (56, 57, 58.5) cm
Sleeve width at upper arm: 14 (15, 15½, 15½)"/35.5 (38, 39.5, 39.5) cm

❀ *Materials*

Paton's *Cotton DK* (light worsted weight; 100% cotton; 1¾ oz/50 g; approx
   116 yd/106 m), 12 (13, 14, 15) balls Cream #6302
Crochet hooks, sizes E/4 and F/5 (3.50 and 3.75 mm) or size needed to obtain
   gauge
Six ½"/13 mm buttons (One World Button Supply Company's *Bone Cowery Shell
   Button Style #NPL 310B* was used on sample garment)

❀ *Gauge*

In Cross Stitch Patt with larger hook, 22 sts and 12 rows = 4"/10 cm.
In Textured Sand Patt with larger hook, 22 sts and 14 rows = 4"/10 cm.
To measure your gauge, make a test swatch as follows: Ch 23 with larger hook.
   Work Cross Stitch Patt on 22 sts for 12 rows. Fasten off.
Piece should measure 4"/10 cm square. **To save time, take time to check gauge.**

Cont in patt as established and dec 1 st each side every row 8 (8, 10, 10) times—78 (82, 86, 90) sts rem.

Cont even until piece measures approx 19 (20, 20½, 21)"/48.5 (51, 52, 53.5) cm from beg, ending after WS row. *Do not ch 2 to turn.*

Shape Neck and Shoulders: Next Row (RS): Slip st into first 6 (6, 7, 7) sts, ch 2, cont in patt across next 14 (16, 17, 19) sts—15 (17, 18, 20) sts total. Ch 2, turn, leaving rest of row unworked.

Next Row: Skip first st, work in patt across next 9 (10, 11, 12) sts, turn, leaving rest of row unworked. *Do not ch 2 to turn.*

Next Row: Slip st into first 5 (6, 6, 7) sts. Fasten off.

For second side of shoulder and neck shaping, with RS facing, skip the middle 38 sts and attach yarn with a slip st to next st and ch 2. Skip first st, work in patt across next 14 (16, 17, 19) sts. *Do not ch 2 to turn.*

Next Row: Slip st into first 6 (7, 7, 8) sts, ch 2, cont patt to end row. Ch 2, turn.

Next Row: Skip first st, work in patt across next 4 (5, 5, 6) sts. Fasten off.

✿ Left Front

With larger hook, ch 55 (59, 63, 67). Beg Cross Stitch Patt, and work even on 54 (58, 62, 66) sts until piece measures approx 8½ (9¼, 9¼, 10)"/ 21.5 (23.5, 23.5, 25.5) cm from beg, ending after Row 1 of patt. Ch 2, turn.

Next Row (RS): Beg Textured Sand Patt. Cont even until piece measures approx 11½ (12, 12, 12½)"/29 (30.5, 30.5, 32) cm from beg, ending after WS row.

Shape Armhole: Next Row (RS): Slip st into first 9 (11, 11, 13) sts, ch 2, cont in patt as established across to end row.

Dec 1 st at armhole edge every row 8 (8, 10, 10) times; **and at the same time,** when piece measures approx 12½ (13½, 14, 14½)"/32 (34.5, 35.5, 37) cm from beg, **Shape Neck** by decreasing 1 st at neck edge every row fourteen times, then every other row four times.

Cont even until piece measures same as back to shoulder, ending after WS row.

Shape Shoulder: Same as first shoulder on back. Fasten off.

✿ Right Front

Work as for left front until piece measures approx 11½ (12, 12, 12½)"/29 (30.5, 30.5, 32) cm from beg, ending after WS row.

Shape Armhole: Next Row (RS): Work across first 46 (48, 52, 54) sts, ch 2, turn, leaving rest of row unworked.

Dec 1 st at armhole edge every row 8 (8, 10, 10) times; **and at the same time,** when piece measures approx 12½ (13½, 14, 14½)"/32 (34.5, 35.5, 37) cm from beg, **Shape Neck** by decreasing 1 st at neck edge every row fourteen times, then every other row four times.

Complete as for left front, **Shaping Shoulder** as for second shoulder on back.

✿ Sleeves

With larger hook, ch 67 (71, 75, 79). Beg Cross Stitch Patt, and work even on 66 (70, 74, 78) sts for one row.

Inc 1 st each side every row 4 (4, 4, 8) times, then every other row 2 (2, 2, 0) times—78 (82, 86, 86) sts.

Cont even until sleeve measures approx 3"/7.5 cm from beg, ending after WS row. *Do not ch 2 to turn.*

Shape Cap: Next Row (RS): Slip st into first 9 (11, 11, 13) sts, ch 2, cont in patt across next 61 (61, 65, 61) sts, ch 2, turn, leaving rest of row unworked.

Dec 1 st each side every other row 0 (2, 2, 4) times, then every row 11 (9, 11, 7) times—40 sts rem. *Do not ch 2 to turn.*

Next Row: Slip st into first 3 sts, ch 2, cont in patt across next 35 sts. *Do not ch 2 to turn.*

Next Row: Slip st into first 3 sts, ch 2, cont in patt across next 31 sts. *Do not ch 2 to turn.*

Next Row: Slip st into first 3 sts, ch 2, cont in patt across next 27 sts. *Do not ch 2 to turn.*

Next Row: Slip st into first 3 sts, ch 2, cont in patt across next 23 sts. Fasten off.

❀ Finishing

Sew shoulder seams.

Front, Back, and Sleeve Lower Edges: With WS facing and smaller hook, attach yarn to first ch of foundation ch and ch 3.

Row 1 (WS): Working into unworked loops of foundation ch, skip first 2 ch, dc into next ch, working over dc just made, dc into the last skipped ch, *skip next ch, dc into next ch, working over last dc made, dc into the skipped ch. Repeat from * across, ending row with dc into last ch. Ch 1, turn.

Row 2: Sc into first 2 sts, *ch 3, slip st into last sc made, sc into next 2 sts. Repeat from * across, ending row with ch 3, slip st into last sc made, sc into next sc, sc into top of ch-3. Fasten off.

Front Bands: With RS facing and smaller hook, attach yarn with a slip st to lower right front edge and ch 1. Work sc along right front opening, around back of neck, and along left front opening, working 2 sc at beg of front neck shapings and dec sc at each shoulder.

Cont in sc until band measures approx ½"/1.5 cm from beg.

Place markers for six evenly spaced buttonholes along right front, making the first ½"/1.5 cm from beg of neck shaping and the last ½"/1.5 cm from lower edge.

Next Row: Cont in sc as before, working (ch 3, skip next 3 sc) where marked.

Cont in sc as before until band measures approx 1"/2.5 cm from beg. Fasten off.

Set in sleeves. Sew sleeve and side seams.

Sew on buttons.

Tweed Striped Cardigan Vest

This cropped accessory will quickly become a wardrobe staple. And with only two stitches used—basic chain stitch and single crochet—it is so easy to make!

ADVANCED BEGINNER

❖ *Sizes*

Small (Medium, Large). Instructions are for smallest size, with changes for other sizes noted in parentheses as necessary.

❖ *Finished Measurements*

Bust: 40 (46, 52)"/101.5 (117, 132) cm
Length: 20 (21, 22)"/51 (53.5, 56) cm

❖ *Materials*

Lion Brand's *Wool-Ease* (worsted weight; 86% acrylic/10% wool/4% rayon
    for colors A and B; 80% acrylic/20% wool for color C; 3 oz/85 g; approx
    197 yd/177 m), 3 (3, 4) skeins Navy Sprinkles #110 (A), 2 (2, 3) skeins Burgundy
    Sprinkles #142 (B), and 2 (2, 3) skeins Natural Heather #098 (C)
Crochet hooks, sizes G/6 and H/8 (4.25 and 5.00 mm) or size needed to obtain
    gauge

❖ *Gauge*

In patt with larger hook, 21 sts and 18 rows = 4"/10 cm.
To measure your gauge, make a test swatch as follows: With larger hook, ch 19.
    Work Linked Sc Patt for 18 rows total. Fasten off.
Piece should measure 3½"/9 cm wide and 4"/10 cm long. **To save time, take time
    to check gauge.**

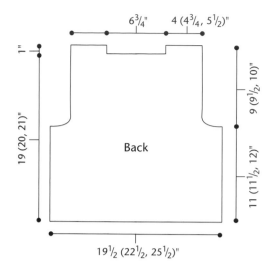

6¾" 4 (4¾, 5½)"
1"
19 (20, 21)"
9 (9½, 10)"
11 (11½, 12)"
Back
19½ (22½, 25½)"

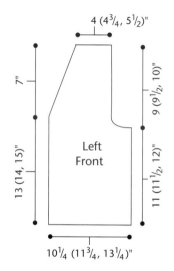

4 (4¾, 5½)"
7"
9 (9½, 10)"
Left Front
13 (14, 15)"
11 (11½, 12)"
10¼ (11¾, 13¼)"

PATTERN NOTES:

- Each sc counts as 1 st.
- Each ch-2 sp counts as 2 sts.
- To change color, work until 2 loops rem on hook; with second color, complete the st; fasten off first color.
- For a description and illustration of any unfamiliar stitch, refer to the back of the book.

❀ Linked Sc Patt

Ch multiple of 4 + 3

Foundation Row (RS): Sc into second ch from hook and into next ch, *ch 2, skip next 2 ch, sc into next 2 ch. Repeat from * across. Ch 1, turn.

Patt Row: Sc into first 2 sc, *ch 2, sc into next 2 sc. Repeat from * across. Ch 1, turn.

Repeat Patt Row for patt.

❀ Stripe Patt

3 rows A

1 row B

3 rows C

1 row B

3 rows A

1 row C

1 row A

1 row B

1 row A

1 row C

Repeat for patt.

❀ Back

With larger hook and A, ch 103 (119, 135). Work Linked Sc Patt in Stripe Patt on 102 (118, 134) sts until piece measures approx 11 (11½, 12)"/28 (29, 30.5) cm from beg, ending after WS row. Fasten off. Turn.

Shape Armholes: Next Row (RS): Cont in Stripe Patt as established, skip first 4 (8, 12) sts, attach yarn with a slip st to next sc, and ch 1. Work Linked Sc Patt across 94 (102, 110) sts, ch 1, turn, leaving rest of row unworked.

Next Row (WS): Work even. Ch 1, turn.

Next Row (RS): Dec sc to combine the first 2 sts. *ch 2, sc into next 2 sc. Repeat from * across until 2 sts rem in row, ending row with dec sc to combine the last 2 sc. Ch 1, turn.

Next Row (WS): Insert hook into first sc and pull up a loop, skip next ch-2 sp, insert hook into next sc and pull up a loop, yarn over and draw it through all 3 loops on hook, sc into next sc, *ch 2, sc into next 2 sc. Repeat from * across until 4 sts rem in row, ending row with insert hook into next sc and pull up a loop, skip next ch-2 sp, insert hook into next st and pull up a loop, yarn over and draw it through all 3 loops on hook. Ch 1, turn.

Repeat last two rows once more—78 (86, 94) sts rem.

Cont even until piece measures approx 19 (20, 21)"/48.5 (51, 53.5) cm from beg, ending after WS row.

Shape Neck: Next Row (WS): Work across first 21 (25, 29) sts, ch 1, turn, leaving rest of row unworked.

Cont even on these shoulder sts until piece measures approx 20 (21, 22)"/51 (53.5, 56) cm from beg. Fasten off.

For second side of neck, with RS facing, skip the middle 36 sts, join yarn with a slip st to next sc and complete as for first side.

✤ Left Front

With larger hook and A, ch 55 (63, 71). Work Linked Sc Patt in Stripe Patt on 54 (62, 70) sts until piece measures approx 11 (11½, 12)"/28 (29, 30.5) cm from beg, ending after WS row. Fasten off. Turn.

Shape Armhole: Next Row (RS): Cont in Stripe Patt as established, skip first 4 (8, 12) sts, attach yarn with a slip st to next sc, and ch 1. Work Linked Sc Patt across to end row. Ch 1, turn.

Next Row (WS): Work even. Ch 1, turn.

Next Row (RS): Dec sc to combine the first 2 sts. *ch 2, sc into next 2 sc. Repeat from * across to end row. Ch 1, turn.

Next Row (WS): Work patt as established until 4 sts rem in row, ending row with insert hook into next sc and pull up a loop, skip next ch-2 sp, insert hook into next st and pull up a loop, yarn over and draw it through all 3 loops on hook. Ch 1, turn.

Repeat last two rows once more—42 (46, 50) sts rem.

Cont even until piece measures approx 13 (14, 15)"/33 (35.5, 38) cm from beg, ending after RS row.

Shape Neck: Next Row (WS): Dec Row 1: Dec sc to combine the first 2 sts, *ch 2, sc into next 2 sc. Repeat from * across to end row. Ch 1, turn.

Dec Row 2: Work patt as established until 4 sts rem in row, ending row with insert hook into next sc and pull up a loop, skip next ch-2 sp, insert hook into next st and pull up a loop, yarn over and draw it through all 3 loops on hook. Ch 1, turn.

Work two rows even.

*Work Dec Rows 1 and 2. Work four rows even. Repeat from * three more times.

Work Dec Row 1 once more.

Cont even until piece measures same as back. Fasten off.

✤ Right Front

Work as for left front until piece measures approx 11 (11½, 12)"/28 (29, 30.5) cm from beg, ending after RS row. Fasten off. Turn.

Shape Armhole: Next Row (WS): Cont in Stripe Patt as established, skip first 4 (8, 12) sts, attach yarn with a slip st to next sc, and ch 1. Work Linked Sc Patt across to end row. Ch 1, turn.

Next Row (RS): Work even. Ch 1, turn.

Next Row (WS): Dec sc to combine the first 2 sts. *ch 2, sc into next 2 sc. Repeat from * across to end row. Ch 1, turn.

Next Row (RS): Work patt as established until 4 sts rem in row, ending row with insert hook into next sc and pull up a loop, skip next ch-2 sp, insert hook into next st and pull up a loop, yarn over and draw it through all 3 loops on hook. Ch 1, turn.

Repeat last 2 rows once more—42 (46, 50) sts rem.

Cont even until piece measures approx 13 (14, 15)"/33 (35.5, 38) cm from beg, ending after WS row.

Shape Neck: Next Row (RS): Dec Row 1: Dec sc to combine the first 2 sts, *ch 2, sc into next 2 sc. Repeat from * across to end row. Ch 1, turn.

Dec Row 2: Work patt as established until 4 sts rem in row, ending row with insert hook into next sc and pull up a loop, skip next ch-2 sp, insert hook into next st and pull up a loop, yarn over and draw it through all 3 loops on hook. Ch 1, turn.

Work two rows even.

*Work Dec Rows 1 and 2 once more. Work four rows even. Repeat from * three more times.

Work Dec Row 1 once more.

Cont even until piece measures same as back. Fasten off.

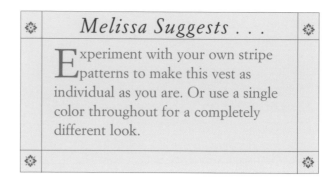

Melissa Suggests . . .

Experiment with your own stripe patterns to make this vest as individual as you are. Or use a single color throughout for a completely different look.

❈ Finishing

Sew shoulder and side seams.

Border: With RS facing and smaller hook, attach A with a slip st to lower right side seam, and ch 1.

Rnd 1 (RS): Work 1 rnd sc around edge, working 3 sc into lower front corners, 2 sc at beg of front neck shaping each side, and dec sc at beg of back neck shaping on each side. Join with a slip st to first sc. Ch 1.

Rnd 2: Work as for last rnd. Join with a slip st to first sc. Fasten off.

Armhole Bands: With RS facing and smaller hook, attach A with a slip st to side seam, and ch 1.

Rnd 1 (RS): Work 84 (88, 90) sc around. Join with a slip st to first sc. Ch 1.

Rnd 2: Work as for last rnd. Join with a slip st to first sc. Fasten off.

Lilac Peek-a-Boo Pullover

Create a sophisticated look by teaming this simple pattern stitch with an exquisite, yet easy-to-make scalloped border.

ADVANCED BEGINNER

❁ *Sizes*

Small (Medium, Large, Extra-Large). Instructions are for smallest size, with changes for other sizes noted in parentheses as necessary.

Finished Measurements

Bust: 40 (42½, 45, 48)"/101.5 (108, 114.5, 122) cm
Length (Including Edging): 21 (21, 22, 22½)"/53.5 (53.5, 56, 57) cm
Sleeve width at upper arm: 18 (18, 19, 20)"/45.5 (45.5, 48.5, 51) cm

❁ *Materials*

Coats and Clark's *Lustersheen* (fingering weight; 100% acrylic; 1⅞ oz/51.5 g;
    approx 150 yd/135 m), 12 (13, 14, 15) balls Lilac #129
Crochet hooks, sizes D/3 and E/4 (3.25 and 3.50 mm) or size needed to obtain
    gauge

❁ *Gauge*

In patt with larger hook, 24 sts and 16 rows = 4"/10 cm.
To measure your gauge, make a test swatch as follows: With larger hook, ch 25.
    Work Peek-a-Boo Patt for 16 rows. Fasten off.
Piece should measure 4"/10 cm square. **To save time, take time to check gauge.**

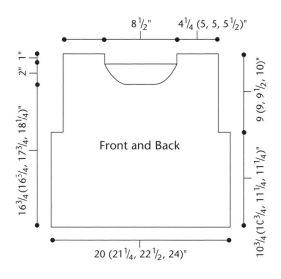

8½" 4¼ (5, 5, 5½)"

2" 1"

16¾ (16¾, 17¾, 18¼)"

Front and Back

9 (9, 9½, 10)"

10¾ (10¾, 11¼, 11¼)"

20 (21¼, 22½, 24)"

18 (18, 19, 20)"

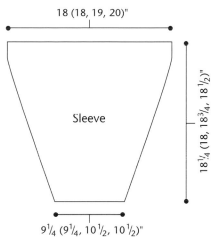

Sleeve

18¼ (18, 18¾, 18½)"

9¼ (9¼, 10½, 10½)"

Note: These measurements do not include the edging.

PATTERN NOTES:

- Each dc and sc counts as 1 st.
- Each turning-ch-3 counts as 1 dc.
- Each ch-2 sp counts as 2 sts.
- To decrease in dc, work until 2 sts rem in row, then work a dec dc to combine the last 2 sts in row. On the next row, work last st into the last dc, not into the top of the turning-ch-3.
- To decrease in sc, work a dec sc to combine the first 2 sts and the last 2 sts of the row.
- To increase, work 2 sts into a st.
- For a description and illustration of any unfamiliar stitch, refer to the back of the book.

❀ Peek-a-Boo Patt

Ch multiple of 8 + 1

Foundation Row (RS): Sc into second ch from hook and into each ch across. Ch 3, turn.

Row 1 (WS): Skip first sc, *dc into next 6 sc, ch 2, skip next 2 sc. Repeat from * across, ending row with dc into last 7 sc. Ch 1, turn.

Row 2: Sc into first 7 dc, *2 sc into next ch-2 sp, sc into next 6 dc. Repeat from * across, ending row with sc into top of turning-ch-3. Ch 3, turn.

Row 3: Skip first sc, dc into next 2 sc, *ch 2, skip next 2 sc, dc into next 6 dc. Repeat from * across, ending row with ch 2, skip next 2 sc, dc into last 3 sc. Ch 1, turn.

Row 4: Sc into first 3 sc, *2 sc into next ch-2 sp, sc into next 6 dc. Repeat from * across, ending row with 2 sc into next ch-2 sp, sc into next 2 dc, sc into top of turning-ch-3. Ch 3, turn.

Repeat Rows 1–4 for patt.

❀ Back

With larger hook, ch 121 (129, 137, 145). Beg Peek-a-Boo Patt, and work even on 120 (128, 136, 144) sts until piece measures approx 10¾ (10¾, 11¼, 11¼"/27.5 (27.5, 28.5, 28.5) cm from beg, ending after Row 2 (Row 2, Row 4, Row 4) of patt. *Do not ch 3 to turn.*

Shape Armholes: Next Row (WS): Slip st into first 9 (9, 13, 13) sc, ch 3, work patt as established across next 103 (111, 111, 119) sts—104 (112, 112, 120) sts rem. Ch 1, turn.

Cont even in patt until armholes measure approx 8 (8, 8½, 9)"/20.5 (20.5, 21.5, 23) cm, ending after RS row.

Shape Neck: Next Row (WS): Work patt across first 26 (30, 30, 34) sts, ch 1, turn.

Cont even on this side until armhole measures approx 9 (9, 9½, 10)"/23 (23, 24, 25.5) cm, ending after RS row. Fasten off.

For second side of neck, with WS facing, skip the middle 52 sts and attach yarn with a slip st to next st and ch 3, work patt across to end row—26 (30, 30, 34) sts.

Complete as for first side.

❀ Front

Work as for back until armholes measure approx 6 (6, 6½, 7)"/15 (15, 16.5, 18) cm, ending after RS row.

Shape Neck: Next Row (WS): Work patt across first 30 (34, 34, 38) sts, ch 1, turn.

Dec 1 st at neck edge next row and then every other row three more times—26 (30, 30, 34) sts rem.

Cont even until this armhole measures approx 9 (9, 9½, 10)"/23 (23, 24, 25.5) cm, ending after RS row. Fasten off.

For second side of neck, with WS facing, skip the middle 44 sts and attach yarn with a slip st to next st and ch 3, work patt across to end row—30 (34, 34, 38) sts.

Complete as for first side.

❧ Sleeves

With larger hook, ch 57 (57, 65, 65). Work Foundation Row of Peek-a-Boo Patt—56 (56, 64, 64) sts.

Cont in patt, and inc 1 st each side every other row 19 (20, 17, 24) times, then every fourth row 7 (6, 8, 4) times—108 (108, 114, 120) sts.

Cont even until sleeve measures 18¼ (18, 18¾, 18½)"/46.5 (45.5, 47.5, 47) cm from beg. Fasten off.

❧ Finishing

Back Lower Edging: With WS facing and smaller hook, attach yarn with a slip st to first ch of foundation ch and ch 3.

Row 1 (WS): Working into unworked loops of foundation ch, skip first ch, dc into next 2 ch, *ch 2, skip next 2 ch, dc into next 6 ch. Repeat from * across, ending row with dc into last 3 ch. Ch 3, turn.

Row 2: Skip first 3 dc, *(3 dc, ch 2, 3 dc) into next ch-2 sp, ch 1. Repeat from * across, ending row with (3 dc, ch 2, 3 dc) into last ch-2 sp, dc into top of ch-3. Ch 3, turn.

Row 3: Skip first 4 dc, *(3 dc, ch 2, 3 dc) into next ch-2 sp, ch 4. Repeat from * across, ending row with (3 dc, ch 2, 3 dc) into last ch-2 sp, dc into top of turning-ch-3. Ch 3, turn.

Row 4: Skip first 4 dc, *(3 dc, ch 3, slip st into third ch from hook, 3 dc) into next ch-2 sp, ch 3, sc into next ch-1 sp 2 rows below, ch 3. Repeat from * across, ending row with (3 dc, ch 3, slip st into third ch from hook, 3 dc) into last ch-2 sp, ch 3, slip st into top of turning-ch-3. Fasten off.

Front and Sleeve Lower Edging: Work as for back lower edging. Sew shoulder seams.

Neckband: With RS facing and smaller hook, attach yarn with a slip st to neck edge of right shoulder seam and ch 1.

Rnd 1: Work 156 sc around neckline.

Rnd 2: Work sc around neckline, making a dec sc each side of beg of front and back neck shaping—152 sc total.

Next Rnd: Work one rnd reverse sc around neckline. Fasten off.

Set in sleeves. Sew sleeve and side seams.

Bobbles 'n' Ribs Pullover

Create this clever version of an Irish classic. Its vertical lines and saddle shoulders compliment everyone's figure.

INTERMEDIATE

❖ *Sizes*

Small (Medium, Large, Extra-Large). Instructions are for smallest size, with changes for other sizes noted in parentheses as necessary.

❖ *Finished Measurements*

Bust: 40 (44, 48½, 53)"/101.5 (112, 123, 134.5) cm
Length: 26 (27, 27½, 28)"/66 (68.5, 70, 71) cm
Sleeve width at underarm: 18 (19, 20, 21)"/45.5 (48.5, 51, 53.5) cm

❖ *Materials*

Lion Brand's *Wool-Ease* (worsted weight; 80% acrylic/20% wool; 3 oz/85 g; approx 197 yd/177 m), 13 (14, 15, 16) skeins Fisherman #99
Crochet hooks, sizes G/6 and H/8 (4.25 and 5.00 mm) or size needed to obtain gauge

❖ *Gauge*

With larger hook in Bobbles 'n' Ribs Patt, 15 sts and 14 rows = 4"/10 cm.
To measure your gauge, make a test swatch as follows: With larger hook, ch 20.
  Work Bobbles 'n' Ribs Patt for 14 rows total. Fasten off.
Piece should measure 5"/12.5 cm wide and 4"/10 cm long. **To save time, take time to check gauge.**

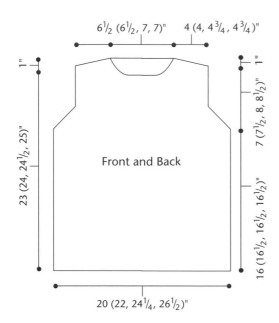

6½ (6½, 7, 7)"   4 (4, 4¾, 4¾)"

1"   1"

Front and Back

23 (24, 24½, 25)"

7 (7½, 8, 8½)"

16 (16½, 16½, 16½)"

20 (22, 24¼, 26½)"

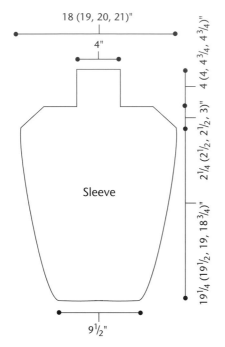

18 (19, 20, 21)"

4"

Sleeve

4 (4, 4¾, 4¾)"

2¼ (2½, 2½, 3)"

19¼ (19½, 19, 18¾)"

9½"

PATTERN NOTES:

- Rope St = (Yarn over, insert hook around post of indicated st from front to back to front, yarn over and pull up a loop, (yarn over and draw it through 2 loops on hook) twice.
- Each turning-ch-2 counts as 1 hdc.
- To decrease in hdc, work until 2 sts rem in row, then work a dec hdc to combine the last 2 sts in row. On the next row, work last st into the last hdc, not into the top of the turning-ch-2.
- To increase, work 2 sts into a st.
- For a description and illustration of any unfamiliar stitch, refer to the back of the book.

❀ Bobbles 'n' Ribs Patt

Ch multiple of 8 + 4

Foundation Row (RS): Hdc into third ch from hook and into next ch, *dc into next ch, hdc into next 3 ch. Repeat from * across. Ch 2, turn.

Row 1 and All WS Rows: Skip first hdc, hdc into each st across, ending row with hdc into top of turning-ch-2. Ch 2, turn.

Row 2: Skip first hdc, hdc into next 2 hdc, *Rope St into next st two rows below, skip hdc behind Rope St just made, hdc into next 3 hdc, Rope St into next st two rows below, skip hdc behind Rope St just made, hdc into next hdc, Bobble, hdc into next hdc. Repeat from * across, ending row with Rope St into next st two rows below, skip hdc behind Rope St just made, hdc into next 2 hdc, hdc into top of turning-ch-2. Ch 2, turn.

Row 4: Skip first hdc, hdc into next 2 hdc, *Rope St into next st two rows below, skip hdc behind Rope St just made, hdc into next 3 hdc. Repeat from * across, ending row with Rope St into next st two rows below, skip hdc behind Rope St just made, hdc into next 2 hdc, hdc into top of turning-ch-2. Ch 2, turn.

Repeat Rows 1–4 for patt.

❧ Sideways Rib Patt

Over any number of ch

Foundation Row: Sc into second ch from hook and into each ch across. Ch 1, turn.

Patt Row: Sc *into the back loop* of each sc across. Ch 1, turn.

Repeat Patt Row.

❀ Back

With larger hook, ch 76 (84, 92, 100). Beg Bobbles 'n' Ribs Patt, and work even on 75 (83, 91, 99) sts until piece measures approx 16 (16½, 16½, 16½)"/ 40.5 (42, 42, 42) cm from beg, ending after WS row. *Do not ch 2 to turn.*

Shape Armholes: Next Row (RS): Slip st into first 4 (7, 7, 10) sts, ch 2, cont in patt across next 68 (70, 78, 80) sts, ch 2, turn.

Cont patt as established, and dec 1 st each side every row 7 (8, 8, 9) times—55 (55, 63, 63) sts rem.

Cont even until piece measures approx 23 (24, 24½, 25)"/58.5 (61, 62, 63.5) cm from beg, ending after WS row. *Do not ch 2 to turn.*

Shape Shoulders: Next Row (RS): Slip st into first 5 (5, 6, 6) sts, ch 2, cont in patt across next 46 (46, 52, 52) sts. *Do not ch 2 to turn.* Turn, leaving rest of row unworked.

Next Row: Slip st into first 5 (5, 6, 6) sts, ch 2, cont in patt across next 38 (38, 42, 42) sts. *Do not ch 2 to turn.* Turn, leaving rest of row unworked.

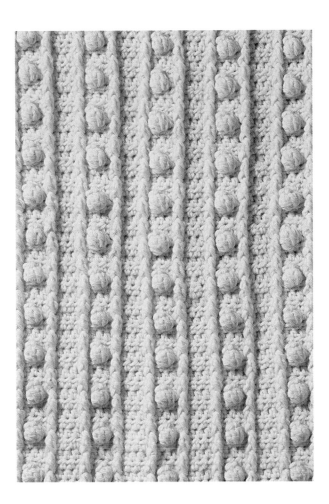

Next Row: Slip st into first 5 sts, ch 2, cont in patt across next 30 (30, 34, 34) sts. *Do not ch 2 to turn.* Turn, leaving rest of row unworked.

Next Row: Slip st into first 4 (4, 5, 5) sts, ch 2, cont in patt across next 24 (24, 26, 26) sts. Fasten off.

❀ Front

Work as for back until piece measures approx 23 (24, 24½, 25)"/58.5 (61, 62, 63.5) cm from beg, ending after WS row. *Do not ch 2 to turn.*

Shape Shoulders and Neck: Next Row (RS): Slip st into first 5 (5, 6, 6) sts, ch 2, cont in patt across next 12 (12, 14, 14) sts, dec hdc to combine next 2 sts, ch 2, turn, leaving rest of row unworked.

Dec 1 hdc at neck edge every row, **and at the same time, Shape Shoulder** as for back. Fasten off.

For second side of neck, with RS facing, skip the middle 17 (17, 19, 19) sts and attach yarn with a slip st to next st and ch 2. Complete as for first side.

❀ Sleeves

With larger hook, ch 36. Beg Bobbles 'n' Ribs Patt on 35 sts, and inc 1 st each side every other row 3 (7, 12, 16) times, then every fourth row 13 (11, 8, 6) times—67 (71, 75, 79) sts. Work even until sleeve measures approx 19¼ (19½, 19, 18¾)"/49 (49.5, 48.5, 47.5) cm from beg, ending after WS row. *Do not ch 2 to turn.*

Shape Armholes: Next Row (RS): Slip st into first 4 (7, 7, 10) sts, ch 2, cont in patt across next 60 (58, 62, 60) sts, ch 2, turn.

Cont patt as established, and dec 1 st each side every row 7 (8, 8, 9) times—47 (43, 47, 43) sts rem. *Do not ch 2 to turn.*

Beg Saddle: Next Row: Slip st into first 17 (15, 17, 15) sts, ch 2, cont in patt as established across next 14 sts. Ch 2, turn, leaving rest of row unworked.

Cont even in patt as established on 15 sts until saddle measures approx 4 (4, 4¾, 4¾)"/10 (10, 12, 12) cm. Fasten off.

❀ Finishing

Sew back and front shoulders to saddle.

Set in sleeves. Sew sleeve and side seams.

Lower Edging: With RS facing and smaller hook, work one rnd of sc evenly around lower edges of body and sleeves. Fasten off.

Neckband: With smaller hook and RS facing, work 77 (77, 81, 81) sc around neckline. Fasten off.

With smaller hook, ch 17. Work Sideways Rib Patt until piece, when slightly stretched, fits around neckline—16 sc each row. Fasten off.

Sew foundation row of neckband to the last row of the neckband. Sewing *through back loops* of each sc, sew neck ribbing into place onto neckline, placing seam at center of back neck.

Tropical Shell

Whip up a fun pullover in bright Caribbean colors using this interesting stitch pattern.

ADVANCED BEGINNER

❀ *Sizes*

Small (Medium, Large, Extra-Large). Instructions are for smallest size, with changes for other sizes noted in parentheses as necessary.

❀ *Finished Measurements*

Bust: 34 (37, 39½, 42)"/86.5 (94, 100.5, 106.5) cm
Length: 20 (21, 21, 22)"/51 (53.5, 53.5, 56) cm

❀ *Materials*

Tahki-Stacy Charles's *Cotton Classic* (heavy worsted weight; 100% cotton; 1¾ oz/ 50 g; approx 108 yd/100 m), 8 (9, 10, 11) hanks White #3001 (A), 1 (1, 2, 2) hanks *each* of Orange #3401 (B), Bright Yellow #3533 (C), Persimmon #3411 (D), and Chartreuse #3723 (E)
Crochet hook, size G/6 (4.25 mm) or size needed to obtain gauge
One ½"/13 mm button (JHB International's *Moonstone Style #71622* was used on sample garment)

❀ *Gauge*

In patt, 18 sts and 14 rows = 4"/10 cm.
To measure your gauge, make a test swatch as follows: With larger hook, ch 19. Work Spiked Patt for 14 rows. Fasten off.
Piece should measure 4"/10 cm square. **To save time, take time to check gauge.**

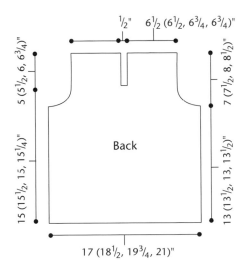

½" 6½ (6½, 6¾, 6¾)"

5 (5½, 6, 6¾)"

7 (7½, 8, 8½)"

Back

15 (15½, 15, 15¼)"

13 (13½, 13, 13½)"

17 (18½, 19¾, 21)"

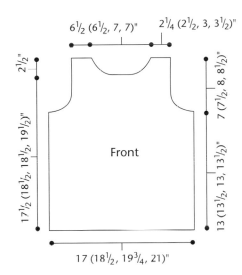

6½ (6½, 7, 7)" 2¼ (2½, 3, 3½)"

2½"

7 (7½, 8, 8½)"

Front

17½ (18½, 18½, 19½)"

13 (13½, 13, 13½)"

17 (18½, 19¾, 21)"

Pattern Notes:

- Long dc = Elongated dc worked into next st two rows below. Always skip the st behind the long dc.
- Each turning-ch-3 counts as 1 dc.
- To decrease in dc, work until 2 sts rem in row, then work a dec dc to combine the last 2 sts in row. On the next row, work last st into the last dc, not into the top of the turning-ch-3.
- To decrease in sc, work a dec sc to combine the first 2 sts and the last 2 sts of the row.
- To increase, work 2 sts into a st.
- To change color, work until 2 loops rem on hook; with second color, complete the st; fasten off first color.
- For a description and illustration of any unfamiliar stitch, refer to the back of the book.

❀ Spiked Patt

Ch multiple of 6 + 1

Foundation Row (WS): Dc into fourth ch from hook and into each ch across. Ch 1, turn.

Row 1 (RS): Sc into each dc across, ending row with sc into third ch of turning-ch-3. Ch 3, turn.

Rows 2, 4, 6, and 8: Skip first sc, dc into each sc across. Ch 1, turn.

Row 3: Sc into first dc, *long dc, sc into next dc, long dc, sc into next 3 dc. Repeat from * across, ending row with long dc, sc into next dc, long dc, sc into top of turning-ch-3. Ch 3, turn.

Row 5: Work as for Row 1.

Row 7: Sc into first 4 dc, *long dc, sc into next dc, long dc, sc into next 3 dc. Repeat from * across, ending row with sc into top of turning-ch-3. Ch 3, turn.

Repeat Rows 1–8 in Color Sequence for patt.

❀ Color Sequence

3 rows A

1 row B

3 rows A

1 row C

3 rows A

1 row D

3 rows A

1 row E

Repeat for patt.

❀ Back

With A, ch 79 (85, 91, 97). Beg Spiked Patt, and work even on 77 (83, 89, 95) sts until piece measures approx 13 (13½, 13, 13½)"/33 (34, 33, 34) cm from beg, ending after WS row. *Do not ch 1 to turn.*

Shape Armholes: Next Row (RS): Slip st into first 7 (8, 8, 9) sts, ch 1, sc into same dc as last slip st, cont in patt as established across next 64 (68, 74, 78) sts, turn, leaving last 6 (7, 7, 8) sts in row unworked—65 (69, 75, 79) sts. *Do not ch 3 to turn.*

Next Row (WS): Slip st into first 4 (4, 4, 5) sts, ch 3, dc into next 58 (60, 60, 62) sts, turn, leaving last 3 (3, 3, 4) sts in row unworked. Ch 1, turn.

Cont in patt as established, and dec 1 st each side every row 5 (5, 5, 4) times—49 (53, 59, 63) sts rem.

Work 1 (1, 1, 0) row even.

Divide for Placket Opening: Next Row (RS): Work across first 23 (25, 28, 30) sts, ch 3, turn, leaving rest of row unworked.

Cont even on 23 (25, 28, 30) sts until armhole measures approx 7 (7½, 8, 8½)"/18 (19, 20.5, 21.5) cm, ending after WS row. Fasten off.

For second side of placket, with RS facing, skip the middle 3 sts; attach yarn with a slip st to next st, and ch 1.

Work even on 23 (25, 28, 30) sts until left side measures same as right side. Fasten off.

❧ Front

Work as for back until piece measures approx 17½ (18½, 18½, 19½)"/44.5 (47, 47, 49.5) cm from beg, ending after WS row.

Shape Neck: Next Row (RS): Work across first 16 (18, 20, 22) sts, ch 3, turn, leaving rest of row unworked. Dec 1 st at neck edge every row six times—10 (12, 14, 16) sts rem this side.

Cont even until this side measures same as back to shoulder. Fasten off.

For second side of neck, with RS facing, skip the middle 17 (17, 19, 19) sts and attach yarn with a slip st to next st and ch 1.

Work even on 10 (12, 14, 16) sts until right side measures same as left side. Fasten off.

❧ Finishing

Sew shoulder seams.

Sew side seams.

Armhole and Lower Edges: With RS facing and A, work two rnds sc evenly around armhole and lower edges, working a dec sc at shoulder seam and top of side seam on the second rnd as necessary. Fasten off.

Neckband: Work as for armhole and lower edges, making a ch-4 buttonloop at top left edge of neck opening, and working a dec sc at both bottom corners of the back placket.

Sew button onto right neck edge opposite buttonloop.

Casual Blazer

You will surprise yourself with how fast you can make this versatile jacket. Combine a textured yarn with a simple stitch. The result? Incredible style!

ADVANCED BEGINNER

❋ *Sizes*

Small (Medium, Large, Extra-Large). Instructions are for smallest size, with changes for other sizes noted in parentheses as necessary.

❋ *Finished Measurements*

Bust (Buttoned): 38½ (41½, 46¼, 49¾)"/97.5 (105.5, 117.5, 126.5) cm
Length: 27 (28, 29, 29½)"/68.5 (71, 73.5, 75) cm
Sleeve width at upper arm: 19¼ (19¼, 20, 21¾)"/49 (49, 51, 55) cm

❋ *Materials*

Lion Brand's *Homespun* (bulky weight; 98% Acrilan® acrylic/2% polyester; 6 oz/ 170 g; approx 185 yd/169 m), 6 (6, 7, 8) skeins Antique #307
Crochet hooks, sizes H/8 (5.00 mm) and K/10.5 (6.50 mm) or size needed to obtain gauge
Six 1½"/38 mm buttons (One World Button Supply Company's *Burnt Horn Leaf Style #NPL 209-38L* was used on sample garment)

❋ *Gauge*

With larger hook, 10 hdc and 8 rows = 4"/10 cm.
To measure your gauge, make a test swatch as follows: Ch 11. **Foundation Row:** Hdc into third ch from hook and into each ch across. Ch 2, turn. **Next Row:** Skip first hdc, hdc into each hdc across, ending row with hdc into top of turning-ch-2. Ch 2, turn. Repeat last row six more times. Fasten off.
Piece should measure 4"/10 cm square. **To save time, take time to check gauge.**

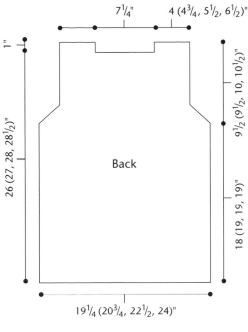

Back

7¼"　　4 (4¾, 5½, 6½)"

1"

26 (27, 28, 28½)"

9½ (9½, 10, 10½)"

18 (19, 19, 19)"

19¼ (20¾, 22½, 24)"

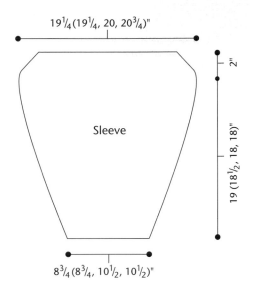

Sleeve

19¼ (19¼, 20, 20¾)"

2"

19 (18½, 18, 18)"

8¾ (8¾, 10½, 10½)"

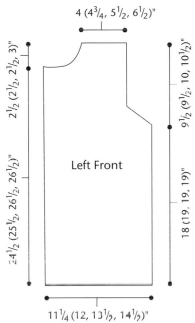

Left Front

4 (4¾, 5½, 6½)"

2½ (2½, 2½, 3)"

24½ (25½, 26½, 26½)"

9½ (9½, 10, 10½)"

18 (19, 19)"

11¼ (12, 13½, 14½)"

PATTERN NOTES:

- Each turning-ch-2 counts as 1 hdc.
- To decrease in hdc, work until 2 sts rem in row, then work a dec hdc to combine the last 2 sts in row. On the next row, work last st into the last hdc, not into the top of the turning-ch-2.
- To increase, work 2 hdc into a st.
- For a description and illustration of any unfamiliar stitch, refer to the back of the book.

❁ Back

With larger hook, ch 49 (53, 57, 61).

Foundation Row: Hdc into third ch from hook and into each ch across—48 (52, 56, 60) hdc total. Ch 2, turn.

Next Row: Skip first hdc, hdc into each hdc across, ending row with hdc into top of turning-ch-2. Ch 2, turn.

Repeat last row until piece measures approx 18 (19, 19, 19)"/45.5 (48.5, 48.5, 48.5) cm from beg. *Do not ch 2 to turn.*

Shape Armholes: Next Row: Slip st into first 2 hdc, ch 2, dec hdc to join next 2 sts, hdc into next 40 (44, 48, 52) hdc, dec hdc to join next 2 sts, hdc into next hdc. Ch 2, turn, leaving turning-ch-2 unworked.

Next Row: Skip first hdc, hdc into next 40 (44, 48, 52) hdc, dec hdc to join next hdc and the turning-ch-2. Ch 2, turn.

Next Row: Skip first dec hdc, dec hdc to join next 2 hdc, hdc into next 36 (40, 44, 48) hdc, dec hdc to join next 2 hdc, hdc into next hdc. Ch 2, turn.

Next Row: Skip first hdc, hdc into next 36 (40, 44, 48) hdc, dec hdc to join last hdc and turning-ch-2. Ch 2, turn.

Next Row: Skip first hdc, hdc into each st across, ending row with hdc into top of turning-ch-2. Ch 2, turn.

Cont even on 38 (42, 46, 50) hdc until piece measures approx 26 (27, 28, 28½)"/66 (68.5, 71, 72.5) cm from beg. Ch 2, turn.

Shape Neck: Place a marker on the side of the fabric which now faces you.

Next Row: Skip first hdc, hdc into next 9 (11, 13, 15) hdc, ch 2, turn, leaving rest of row unworked.

Next Row: Work even. Fasten off.

For second side of neck shaping, with the marked side of fabric facing you, skip the middle 18 hdc and attach yarn with a slip st to next st and ch 2, and work hdc into each st across to end row—10 (12, 14, 16) hdc total. Ch 2, turn.

Next Row: Work even. Fasten off.

❀ Pocket Linings (Make two)

With larger hook, ch 17.

Foundation Row: Hdc into third ch from hook and into each ch across—16 hdc total. Ch 2, turn.

Next Row: Skip first hdc, hdc into each hdc across, ending row with hdc into top of turning-ch-2. Ch 2, turn.

Repeat last row until lining measures approx 6"/15 cm from beg. Fasten off.

❀ Left Front

With larger hook, ch 29 (31, 35, 37).

Foundation Row: Hdc into third ch from hook and into each ch across—28 (30, 34, 36) hdc total. Ch 2, turn.

Next Row: Skip first hdc, hdc into each hdc across, ending row with hdc into top of turning-ch-2. Ch 2, turn.

Repeat last row until piece measures approx 7"/ 18 cm from beg. Ch 2, turn.

Place Pocket Lining: Next Row: Skip first hdc, hdc into next 5 (6, 8, 9) hdc, hdc across 16 hdc from pocket lining, skip next 16 hdc on front, work last 6 (7, 9, 10) hdc to end row.

Cont even on 28 (30, 34, 36) hdc until piece measures approx 18 (19, 19, 19)"/45.5 (48.5, 48.5, 48.5) cm from beg. *Do not ch 2 to turn.*

Shape Armhole: Next Row: Slip st into first 2 hdc, ch 2, dec hdc to join next 2 sts, hdc into next 24 (26, 30, 32) hdc to end row. Ch 2, turn.

Next Row: Skip first hdc, hdc into next 23 (25, 29, 31) hdc, dec hdc to join next hdc and the turning-ch-2. Ch 2, turn.

Next Row: Skip first dec hdc, dec hdc to join next 2 hdc, work 22 (24, 28, 30) hdc to end row. Ch 2, turn.

Next Row: Skip first hdc, hdc into next 21 (23, 27, 29) hdc, dec hdc to join next 2 sts. Ch 2, turn.

Next Row: Skip first hdc, hdc into each st across, ending row with hdc into top of turning-ch-2. Ch 2, turn.

Cont even on 23 (25, 29, 31) hdc until piece measures approx 24½ (25½, 26½, 26½)"/62 (65, 67.5, 67.5) cm from beg, ending on the side opposite armhole shaping. *Do not ch 2 to turn.*

Shape Neck: Next Row: Slip st into first 10 (10, 12, 12) hdc, ch 2, dec hdc to join next 2 hdc, work 11 (13, 15, 17) hdc to end row. Ch 2, turn.

Next Row: Skip first hdc, hdc into next 10 (12, 14, 16) hdc, dec hdc to join next dec hdc and the turning-ch-2. Ch 2, turn.

Next Row: Skip first dec hdc, dec hdc to join next 2 hdc, work 9 (11, 13, 15) hdc to end row. Ch 2, turn.

Next Row: Skip first hdc, hdc into next 8 (10, 12, 14) hdc, dec hdc to join next hdc and the turning-ch-2—10 (12, 13, 16) sts. Ch 2, turn.

Next Row: Skip first hdc, hdc into each st across, ending row with hdc into top of turning-ch-2. Fasten off.

Place markers for six evenly spaced buttons along the front edge, making the first one 4"/10 cm down from neck and the last one ½"/1.5 cm up from lower edge.

❖ Right Front

Work as for left front, except make six 2-st buttonholes on WS rows opposite markers and armhole shaping as follows.

Buttonhole Rows: Work until 4 sts rem in row, ch 2, skip next 2 hdc, hdc into next hdc, hdc into top of turning-ch-2. Ch 2, turn.

On subsequent rows, make 2 hdc into the ch-2 space from previous row.

❖ Sleeves

With larger hook, ch 23 (23, 27, 27).

Foundation Row: Hdc into third ch from hook and into each ch across—22 (22, 26, 26) hdc total. Ch 2, turn.

Next Row: Skip first hdc, hdc into each hdc across, ending row with hdc into top of turning-ch-2. Ch 2, turn.

Cont working hdc, and inc 1 hdc each side every other row 9 (9, 8, 10) times, then every fourth row 4 (4, 4, 3) times—48 (48, 50, 52) hdc total.

Cont even until sleeve measures approx 19 (18½, 18, 18)"/48.5 (47, 45.5, 45.5) cm from beg.

Shape Cap: Work same as first four rows of back armhole shaping. Fasten off.

❖ Finishing

Sew shoulder seams.

Pocket Edgings: With RS facing and smaller hook, attach yarn with a slip st to top of pocket opening and ch 1. Work two rows sc along top of pocket. Fasten off.

Sew sides of pocket trim to front. Sew pocket linings to WS of front.

Front Edges: With RS facing and smaller hook, work two rows sc along each front edge between lower edge and neck shaping. Fasten off.

Collar: With larger hook, ch 12.

Foundation Row: Sc into second ch from hook and into each ch across. Ch 1, turn.

Next Row: Sc *into the back loop* of each sc across. Ch 1, turn.

Repeat last row until collar measures approx 22 (22, 23, 24)"/56 (56, 58.5, 61) cm from beg. Fasten off.

Sew collar into place along neckline, beg and end 2"/5 cm from front edges.

Set in sleeves. Sew sleeve and side seams.

Sew on buttons.

Citrus Pullover

Refresh your summer wardrobe with a sporty V-neck sweater. Here, simple stripes create irresistible flashes of color across a crisp white background.

ADVANCED BEGINNER

❈ *Sizes*

Small (Medium, Large, Extra-Large). Instructions are for smallest size, with changes for other sizes noted in parentheses as necessary.

❈ *Finished Measurements*

Bust: 38 (41½, 45, 48½)"/96.5 (105.5, 114.5, 123) cm
Length: 24½ (25, 25, 25½)"/62 (63.5, 63.5, 65) cm
Sleeve width at upper arm: 13 (14, 14, 15)"/33 (35.5, 35.5, 38) cm

❈ *Materials*

Tahki-Stacy Charles's *Cotton Classic* (heavy worsted weight; 100% cotton; 1¾ oz/
    50 g; approx 108 yd/100 m), 9 (10, 11, 12) hanks White #3001 (A), 2 (3, 3, 4)
    hanks each of Bright Yellow #3533 (B), Persimmon #3411 (C), Chartreuse
    #3723 (D), and Orange #3401 (E)
Crochet hook, size G/6 (4.25 mm) or size needed to obtain gauge

❈ *Gauge*

In patt, 18 sts and 16 rows = 4"/10 cm.
To measure your gauge, make a test swatch as follows: Ch 22. Work Textured
    Striped Rib Patt for 16 rows. Fasten off.
Piece should measure 4½"/11.5 cm wide and 4"/10 cm long. **To save time, take
    time to check gauge.**

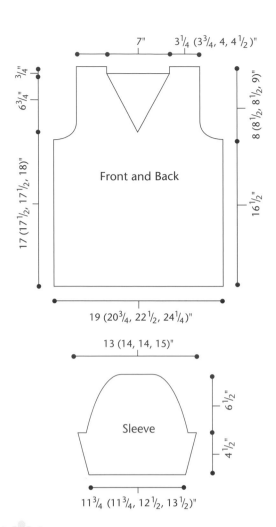

7"   3¼ (3¾, 4, 4½)"

¾"

6¾"

8 (8½, 8½, 9)"

17 (17½, 17½, 18)"

16½"

Front and Back

19 (20¾, 22½, 24¼)"

13 (14, 14, 15)"

6½"

Sleeve

4½"

11¾ (11¾, 12½, 13½)"

❧ Pattern Notes:

- Unless noted otherwise, always skip the st behind the FPDC.
- Triple dec sc = (Insert hook into next st, yarn over and pull up a loop) three times, yarn over and draw it through all 4 loops on hook.
- Each turning-ch-3 counts as 1 dc.
- To decrease in dc, work until 2 sts rem in row, then work a dec dc to combine the last 2 sts in row. On the next row, work last st into the last dc, not into the top of the turning-ch-3.
- To decrease in sc, work a dec sc to combine the first 2 sts and the last 2 sts of the row.
- To increase, work 2 sts into a st.
- Reverse sc = Working *from left to right,* sc into each sc across.
- To change color, work until 2 loops rem on hook; with second color, complete the st; fasten off first color.
- For a description and illustration of any unfamiliar stitch, refer to the back of the book.

❧ Textured Striped Rib Patt

Ch multiple of 4 + 2

Foundation Row (RS): Sc into second ch from hook and into each ch across. Ch 3, turn.

Row 1 (WS): Skip first sc, *dc into each st across. Ch 1, turn.

Row 2: Sc into first dc and into each dc across, ending row with sc into top of turning-ch-3. Ch 1, turn.

Row 3: Sc into each sc across. Ch 1, turn.

Row 4: Sc into first 2 sc, *FPDC, skip sc behind FPDC just made, sc into next 3 sc. Repeat from * across, ending row with FPDC, skip sc behind FPDC just made, sc into last 2 sc. Ch 3, turn.

Repeat Rows 1–4 in Color Sequence for patt.

❧ Color Sequence

2 rows A

2 rows B

2 rows A

2 rows C

2 rows A

2 rows D

2 rows A

2 rows E

Repeat for patt.

❧ Back

With A, ch 86 (94, 102, 110). Beg Textured Striped Rib Patt, and work even on 85 (93, 101, 109) sts until piece measures approx 16½"/42 cm from beg, ending after WS row. Fasten off.

Shape Armholes: Next Row (RS): Skip first 5 (6, 8, 9) sts, attach yarn with a slip st to next st and ch 1, cont in patt as established across next 75 (81, 85, 91) sts, turn, leaving last 5 (6, 8, 9) sts in row unworked.

Dec 1 st each side every row 7 (8, 9, 9) times—61 (65, 67, 73) sts rem.

Cont in patt as established until armholes measure approx 7 (7½, 7½, 8)"/18 (19, 19, 20.5) cm, ending after a WS row worked with A.

Shape Neck: Next Row (RS): Work across first 15 (17, 18, 21) sts, turn, leaving rest of row unworked.

Cont even on these 15 (17, 18, 21) sts until armhole measures approx 8 (8½, 8½, 9)"/20.5 (21.5, 21.5, 23) cm. Fasten off.

For second side of neck, with RS facing, skip the middle 31 sts, join yarn with a slip st to next st and work patt across 15 (17, 18, 21) sts to end row. Complete as for first side.

❀ Front

Work as for back until piece measures approx 17 (17½, 17½, 18)"/43 (44.5, 44.5, 45.5) cm from beg, ending after WS row. Mark center st.

Shape Neck: Next Row (RS): Work a dec st at armhole edge as before, work across to 2 sts before marked st, work a dec st, turn, leaving rest of row unworked.

Cont armhole shaping as for back, and dec 1 st at neck edge every other row fourteen more times.

Cont even on 15 (17, 18, 21) sts until piece measures same as back to shoulder. Fasten off.

For second side of neck, with RS facing, skip the middle st, join yarn with a slip st to next st, work a dec st, cont in patt across, working a dec st at armhole edge; turn. Complete as for first side.

❀ Sleeves

With A, ch 54 (54, 58, 62). Work Foundation Row of Textured Striped Rib Patt—53 (53, 57, 61) sts.

Cont in patt, and inc 1 st each side every other row 0 (2, 0, 0) times, then every fourth row three times—59 (63, 63, 67) sts.

Cont even until sleeve measures approx 4½"/11.5 cm from beg, ending after WS row. Fasten off.

Shape Cap: Next Row (RS): Skip first 5 (6, 8, 9) sts, attach yarn with a slip st to next st and ch 1, cont in patt as established across next 49 (51, 47, 49) sts, turn, leaving last 5 (6, 8, 9) sts in row unworked.

Dec 1 st each side every other row 11 (10, 13, 13) times, then every row 4 (6, 0, 0) times—19 (19, 21, 23) sts rem. Fasten off.

❀ Finishing

Sew shoulder seams.

Neckband: With RS facing, attach A with a slip st to neck edge of left shoulder seam and ch 1.

Rnd 1: Work sc evenly around neckline, working triple dec sc at center front of neck and dec sc at beg of neck shaping on each side. Join with a slip st to first sc.

Rnds 2 and 3: Work same as Rnd 1.

Rnd 4: Work reverse sc around. Join with a slip st to first sc. Fasten off.

Set in sleeves. Sew sleeve and side seams.

Sleeve and Lower Edges: With RS facing, attach A with a slip st to seam and ch 1.

Rnd 1: Work sc evenly around. Join with a slip st to first sc.

Rnd 2: Work reverse sc around. Join with a slip st to first sc. Fasten off.

Dressy Chenille Cardigan

Showcase your love for crochet with this elegant design. Its pretty trim and fancy button closure make it perfect for special occasions.

INTERMEDIATE

❀ Sizes

Small (Medium, Large, Extra-Large). Instructions are for smallest size, with changes for other sizes noted in parentheses as necessary.

❀ Finished Measurements

Bust (Buttoned): 35½ (39½, 43, 46)"/90 (100.5, 109, 117) cm
Length (Including Edging): 20½ (21½, 22½, 23½)"/52 (54.5, 57, 59.5) cm

❀ Materials

Lion Brand's *Chenille Sensations* (heavy worsted weight; 100% Acrilan® acrylic; 1⅖ oz/40 g; approx 87 yd/80 m), 15 (17, 19, 21) skeins Black #153
Crochet hook, size H/8 (5.00 mm) or size needed to obtain gauge
One 1"/25 mm button (JHB International's *Femme Fatale Style #31158* was used on sample garment)

❀ Gauge

In Lace Patt, four 3-dc groups measure 3¼"/8.5 cm wide.
In solid sc, 16 sts and 18 rows = 4"/10 cm.
To measure your gauge, make a test swatch as follows: Ch 17. Work Lace Patt for 12 rows. Fasten off.
Piece should measure 4½"/11.5 cm wide and 4"/10 cm long. **To save time, take time to check gauge.**

Pattern Notes:

- Each ch-3 counts as 3 sts.
- For a description and illustration of any unfamiliar stitch, refer to the back of the book.

❧ Lace Patt

Ch multiple of 3 + 2

Foundation Row (WS): Sc into second ch from hook, *ch 3, skip next 2 ch, sc into next ch. Repeat from * across. Ch 3, turn.

Row 1 (RS): Dc into first sc, *sc into next ch-3 sp, 3 dc into next sc. Repeat from * across, ending row with sc into next ch-3 sp, 2 dc into last sc. Ch 1, turn.

Row 2: Sc into first dc, *ch 3, skip next 3 sts, sc into next dc. Repeat from * across, ending row with ch 3, skip next 3 sts, sc into top of turning-ch-3. Ch 3, turn.

Repeat Rows 1 and 2 for patt.

❧ Back

Ch 65 (71, 77, 83). Work Foundation Row of Lace Patt—21 (23, 25, 27) ch-3 spaces across.

Cont patt until piece measures approx 11¼ (12¼, 12¼, 13¼)"/28.5 (31, 31, 33.5) cm from beg, ending after WS row. *Do not ch 3 to turn.*

Shape Armholes: Next Row (RS): Slip st into first 9 sts, ch 3, dc into same sc as last slip st, *sc into next ch-3 sp, 3 dc into next sc. Repeat from * 15 (17, 19, 21) more times, then work sc into next ch-3 sp, 2 dc into next sc, ch 1, turn, leaving rest of row unworked.

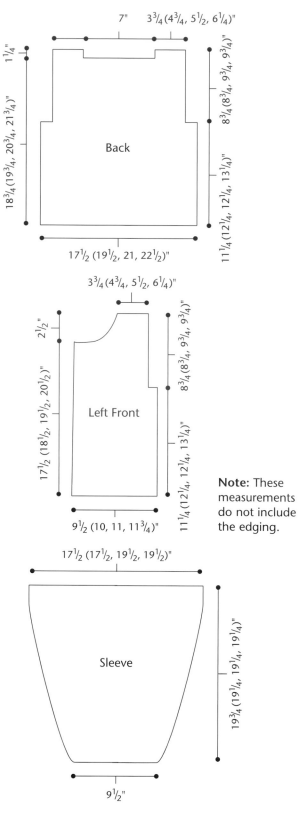

Note: These measurements do not include the edging.

Cont even in Lace Patt until armholes measure approx 7½ (7½, 8½, 8½)"/19 (19, 21.5, 21.5) cm, ending after WS row. Ch 3, turn.

Shape Neck: Next Row (RS): Dc into first sc, *sc into next ch-3 sp, 3 dc into next sc. Repeat from * three more times, then work sc into next ch-3 sp, 2 dc into next sc, ch 1, turn, leaving rest of row unworked.

Work even for three more rows. Fasten off.

For second side of neck shaping, with RS facing, skip the middle 9 ch-3 spaces and attach yarn with a slip st to next sc, ch 3, dc into same sc as last slip st, *sc into next ch-3 sp, 3 dc into next sc. Repeat from * across to end row.

Complete same as first side.

❀ Left Front

Ch 35 (38, 41, 44). Work Foundation Row of Lace Patt—11 (12, 13, 14) ch-3 spaces across.

Cont patt until piece measures approx 11¼ (12¼, 12¼, 13¼)"/28.5 (31, 31, 33.5) cm from beg, ending after WS row. *Do not ch 3 to turn.*

Shape Armhole: Next Row (RS): Slip st into first 9 sts, ch 3, dc into same sc as last slip st, *sc into next ch-3 sp, 3 dc into next sc. Repeat from * across, ending row with sc into next ch-3 sp, 2 dc into last sc. Ch 1, turn.

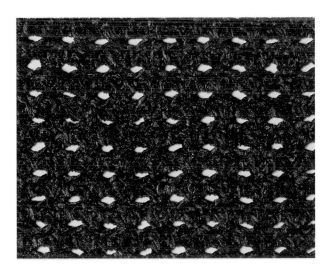

Cont even in Lace Patt until armhole measures approx 6¼ (6¼, 7¼, 7¼)"/16 (16, 18.5, 18.5) cm, ending after RS row. *Do not ch 1 to turn.*

Shape Neck: Next Row (WS): Slip st into first 4 sts, sc into next dc, *ch 3, skip next 3 sts, sc into next dc. Repeat from * across, ending row with ch 3, skip next 3 sts, sc into top of turning-ch-3. Ch 3, turn.

Next Row: Dc into first sc, *sc into next ch-3 sp, 3 dc into next sc. Repeat from * across, ending row with sc into next ch-3 sp, slip st into last sc from previous row. *Do not ch 1 to turn.*

Next Row: Slip st into first 7 sts, sc into next st, *ch 3, skip next 3 sts, sc into next dc. Repeat from * across, ending row with ch 3, skip next 3 sts, sc into top of turning-ch-3. Ch 3, turn.

Repeat last two rows once more.

Cont in patt until piece measures same as back to shoulder. Fasten off.

❀ Right Front

Work as for left front until piece measures approx 11¼ (12¼, 12¼, 13¼)"/28.5 (31, 31, 33.5) cm from beg, ending after WS row.

Shape Armhole: Next Row (RS): Work Lace Patt as established across until 8 sts rem in row. Ch 3, turn, leaving last 8 sts of row unworked.

Cont even in Lace Patt until armhole measures approx 6¼ (6¼, 7¼, 7¼)"/16 (16, 18.5, 18.5) cm, ending after RS row. Ch 1, turn.

Shape Neck: Next Row (WS): Sc into first dc, *ch 3, skip next 3 sts, sc into next dc. Repeat from * across until 4 sts rem in row. Ch 1, turn, leaving last 4 sts of row unworked.

Next Row: Sc into next ch-3 sp, *3 dc into next sc, sc into next ch-3 sp. Repeat from * across, ending row with 2 dc into last st. Ch 1, turn.

Next Row: Sc into first dc, *ch 3, skip next 3 sts, sc into next dc. Repeat from * across until 7 sts rem in row. Ch 1, turn, leaving last 7 sts of row unworked.

Repeat last two rows once more.

Complete as for left front.

❀ Sleeves

Ch 35. Work Foundation Row of Lace Patt—11 ch-3 spaces across.

Cont even until piece measures approx 1¼ (2¼, 2¼, 3¼)"/3 (5.5, 5.5, 8.5) cm from beg, ending after WS row.

Next Row (RS): 2 dc into first sc, *sc into next ch-3 sp, 3 dc into next sc. Repeat from * across. Ch 1, turn.

Next Row: Sc into first dc, ch 1, sc into next dc, *ch 3, skip next 3 sts, sc into next dc. Repeat from * across, ending row with ch 1, sc into top of turning-ch-3. Ch 3, turn.

Next Row: Dc into first sc, sc into ch-1 sp, *3 dc into next sc, sc into next ch-3 sp. Repeat from * across ending row with 3 dc into next sc, sc into ch-1 sp, 2 dc into last sc. Ch 1, turn.

Next Row: Work same as Row 2 of Lace Patt.

Next 6 (6, 4, 4) Rows: Work same as Rows 1 and 2 of Lace Patt.

Repeat last 10 (10, 8, 8) rows 4 (4, 5, 5) more times.

Cont even until sleeve measures approx 19¾ (19¼, 19¼, 19¼)"/50 (49, 49, 49) cm from beg, ending after WS row. Fasten off.

❀ Finishing

Back Lower Border: With RS facing, attach yarn with a slip st to first sc. Working along opposite side of foundation ch, sc into each ch across. Ch 1, turn.

Next Row: Sc into each sc across. Ch 1, turn.

Next Row: Sc into first sc, *ch 3, 2 dc into same place as last sc, skip next 2 sc, sc into next sc. Repeat from * across. Fasten off.

Front Lower Borders: Work as for back lower border.

Sew shoulder seams.

Set in sleeves. Sew sleeve and side seams.

Sleeve Lower Borders: Work as for back lower border.

Front Edges: With RS facing, attach yarn to lower right front edge and ch 1. Work two rows of sc along right front edge, around neckline, and down left front edge, making one ch-9 buttonhole loop at right front neck. Fasten off.

Sew on button.

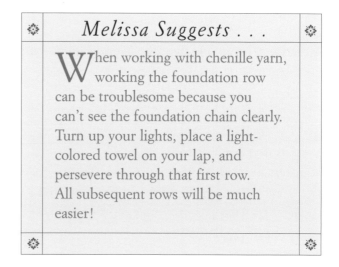

❀ *Melissa Suggests . . .* ❀

When working with chenille yarn, working the foundation row can be troublesome because you can't see the foundation chain clearly. Turn up your lights, place a light-colored towel on your lap, and persevere through that first row. All subsequent rows will be much easier!

Clusters-and-Lace Cardigan

Add a touch of Victorian romance to any outfit with this openwork jacket. Its delicate collar and edging are fun and easy to crochet.

INTERMEDIATE

❖ *Sizes*

Small (Medium, Large, Extra-Large). Instructions are for smallest size, with changes for other sizes noted in parentheses as necessary.

❖ *Finished Measurements*

Bust (Buttoned): 38 (42½, 46½, 51¼)"/96.5 (108, 118.5, 130) cm
Length (Including Edging): 20 (21, 21, 22)"/51 (53.5, 53.5, 56) cm
Sleeve width at upper arm: 15½ (15½, 16½, 16½)"/39.5 (39.5, 42, 42) cm

❖ *Materials*

JCA/Reynolds's *Sedona* (sport weight; 100% cotton; 1¾ oz/ 50 g; approx
   111 yd/102 m), 18 (19, 20, 21) skeins Sugar #101
Crochet hooks, sizes E/4 and F/5 (3.50 and 3.75 mm) or size needed to obtain
   gauge
Seven ¾"/20 mm buttons (One World Button Supply Company's *Bone Pinwheels
   Style #NPL 129,* was used on sample garment)

❖ *Gauge*

In patt with larger hook, 22 sts = 4"/10 cm wide.
To measure your gauge, make a test swatch as follows: Ch 26 with larger hook.
   Work Clusters-and-Lace Patt for 10 rows. Fasten off.
Piece should measure 4¼"/11 cm wide and 3"/7.5 cm long. **To save time, take time
   to check gauge.**

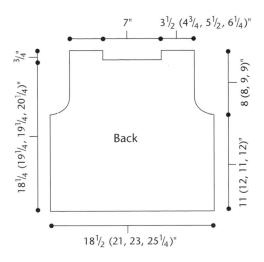

7"　　3½ (4¾, 5½, 6¼)"

¾"

8 (8, 9, 9)"

18¼ (19¼, 19¼, 20¼)"

Back

11 (12, 11, 12)"

18½ (21, 23, 25¼)"

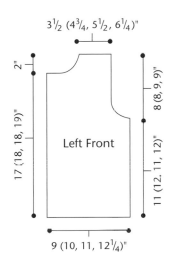

3½ (4¾, 5½, 6¼)"

2"

8 (8, 9, 9)"

17 (18, 18, 19)"

Left Front

11 (12, 11, 12)"

9 (10, 11, 12¼)"

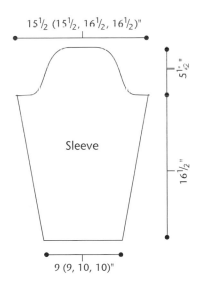

15½ (15½, 16½, 16½)"

5½"

Sleeve

16½"

9 (9, 10, 10)"

Note: These measurements do not include the edging.

Pattern Notes:

- 4-dc cluster = (Yarn over, insert hook into indicated st and pull up a loop, yarn over and draw it through 2 loops) four times, yarn over and draw it through all 5 loops on hook.
- 3-sc dec = (Insert hook into next indicated st and draw up a loop) three times, yarn over and draw it through all 4 loops on hook.
- 3-dc dec = (Yarn over, insert hook into next indicated st, yarn over and pull up a loop, yarn over and draw it through 2 loops on hook) three times, yarn over and draw it through all 4 loops on hook.
- 4-dc dec = (Yarn over, insert hook into next indicated st, yarn over and pull up a loop, yarn over and draw it through 2 loops on hook) three times, yarn over and draw it through all 5 loops on hook.
- For a description and illustration of any unfamiliar stitch, refer to the back of the book.

❀ Clusters-and-Lace Patt

Ch multiple of 6 + 2

Foundation Row 1 (RS): Sc into second ch from hook and into each ch across. Ch 1, turn.

Foundation Row 2: Sc into first 2 sc, *ch 5, skip next 3 sc, sc into next sc, 4-dc cluster into next sc, sc into next sc. Repeat from * across, ending row with ch 5, skip next 3 sc, sc into last 2 sc. Ch 3, turn.

Row 1 (RS): Skip first sc, dc into next sc, *3 sc into next ch-5 sp, dc into next sc, dc into next 4-dc cluster, dc into next sc. Repeat from * across, ending row with 3 sc into next ch-5 sp, dc into last 2 sc. Ch 1, turn.

Row 2: Sc into first 2 dc, *ch 5, skip next 3 sc, sc into next dc, 4-dc cluster into next dc, sc into next dc. Repeat from * across, ending row with ch 5, skip next 3 sc, sc into next dc, sc into top of turning-ch-3. Ch 3, turn.

Repeat Rows 1 and 2 for patt.

❀ Back

With larger hook, ch 104 (116, 128, 140). Beg Clusters-and-Lace Patt, and work even on 103 (115, 127, 139) sts until piece measures approx 11 (12, 11, 12)"/28 (30.5, 28, 30.5) cm from beg, ending after RS row. *Do not ch 1 to turn.*

Shape Armholes: Next Row (WS): Slip st into first 7 sts, ch 1, sc into same dc as last slip st, sc into next dc, *ch 5, skip next 3 sc, sc into next dc, 4-dc cluster into next dc, sc into next dc. Repeat from * across until 7 sts rem in row, ending row with sc into next st. Ch 3, turn, leaving rest of row unworked.

Next Row: Skip first sc, dc into next sc, *3 sc into next ch-5 sp, dc into next sc, dc into next 4-dc cluster, dc into next sc. Repeat from * across, ending row with 3 sc into next ch-5 sp, dc into last 2 sc. Ch 1, turn.

Next Row: 3-sc dec to combine the first 2 dc and the next sc, ch 3, *sc into next dc, 4-dc cluster into next dc, sc into next dc, ch 5, skip next 3 sc. Repeat from * across, ending row with sc into next dc, 4-dc cluster into next dc, sc into next dc, ch 3, skip next 2 sc, 3-sc dec to combine the next sc, the next dc, and the turning-ch-3. Ch 3, turn.

Next Row: 3-dc dec to combine the ch-3 sp, the next sc, and the next 4-dc cluster, dc into next sc, *3 sc into next ch-5 sp, dc into next sc, dc into next 4-dc cluster, dc into next sc. Repeat from * across, ending row with 3 sc into next ch-5 sp, dc into next sc, 4-dc dec to combine the next 4-dc cluster, the next sc, the next ch-3 sp, and the 3-sc dec. Ch 1, turn.

Next Row: Sc into 4-dc dec and into next dc, *ch 5, skip next 3 sc, sc into next dc, 4-dc cluster into next dc, sc into next dc. Repeat from * across, ending row with ch 5, skip next 3 sc, dec sc to combine next 2 dc, sc into top of turning-ch-3. Ch 3, turn.

Cont even in Clusters-and-Lace Patt until piece measures approx 18¼ (19¼, 19¼, 20¼)"/46.5 (49, 49, 51.5) cm from beg, ending after RS row. Ch 1, turn.

Shape Neck: Next Row (WS): Sc into first 2 dc, (ch 5, skip next 3 sc, sc into next dc, 4-dc cluster into next dc, sc into next dc) 3 (4, 5, 6) times, ending row with ch 5, skip next 3 sc, sc into next dc. Ch 4, turn, leaving rest of row unworked.

Next Row: Skip first sc, sc into next ch-5 sp, *dc into next sc, dc into next 4-dc cluster, dc into next sc, 3 sc into next ch-5 sp. Repeat from * across, ending row with dc into last 2 sc. Fasten off.

For second side of neck shaping, with WS facing and larger hook, skip the middle 31 sts and attach yarn with a slip st to next dc, and ch 1. Sc into same dc as the slip st, *ch 5, skip next 3 sc, sc into next dc, 4-dc cluster into next dc, sc into next dc. Repeat from * across, ending row with ch 5, skip next 3 sc, sc into next dc, sc into top of turning-ch. Ch 3, turn.

Next Row: Skip first sc, dc into next sc, *3 sc into next ch-5 sp, dc into next sc, dc into next 4-dc cluster, dc into next sc. Repeat from * across, ending row with insert hook under next ch-5 sp and pull up a loop, yarn over hook twice, insert hook into last sc and pull up a loop, (yarn over and draw it through 2 loops on hook) twice, yarn over and draw it through all 3 loops on hook. Fasten off.

❀ Left Front

With larger hook, ch 50 (56, 62, 68). Beg Clusters-and-Lace Patt, and work even on 49 (55, 61, 67) sts until piece measures approx 11 (12, 11, 12)"/28 (30.5, 28, 30.5) cm from beg, ending after RS row. Ch 1, turn.

Shape Armhole: Next Row (WS): Work across until 7 sts rem in row, ending row with sc into next st. Ch 3, turn, leaving rest of row unworked.

Next Row: Skip first sc, dc into next sc, *3 sc into next ch-5 sp, dc into next sc, dc into next 4-dc cluster, dc into next sc. Repeat from * across, ending row with 3 sc into next ch-5 sp, dc into last 2 sc. Ch 1, turn.

Next Row: Sc into first 2 dc, ch 5, skip next 3 sc, *sc into next dc, 4-dc cluster into next dc, sc into next dc, ch 5, skip next 3 sc. Repeat from * across, ending row with sc into next dc, 4-dc cluster into next dc, sc into next dc, ch 3, skip next 2 sc, 3-sc dec to combine the next sc, the next dc, and the turning-ch-3. Ch 3, turn.

Next Row: 3-dc dec to combine the ch-3 sp, the next sc, and the next 4-dc cluster, dc into next sc, *3 sc into next ch-5 sp, dc into next sc, dc into next 4-dc cluster, dc into next sc. Repeat from * across, ending row with 3 sc into next ch 5 sp, dc into last 2 sc. Ch 1, turn.

Next Row: Sc into the first 2 dc, *ch 5, skip next 3 sc, sc into next dc, 4-dc cluster into next dc, sc into next dc. Repeat from * across, ending row with ch 5, skip next 3 sc, dec sc to combine next 2 dc, sc into top of turning-ch-3. Ch 3, turn.

Cont even in Clusters-and-Lace Patt until piece measures approx 17 (18, 18, 19)"/43 (45.5, 45.5, 48.5) cm from beg, ending after RS row. *Do not ch 1 to turn.*

Shape Neck: Next Row (WS): Slip st into first 7 sts, ch 1, sc into same dc as last slip st, sc into next dc, *ch 5, skip next 3 sc, sc into next dc, 4-dc cluster into next dc, sc into next dc. Repeat from * across, ending row with ch 5, skip next 3 sc, sc into last dc and turning-ch. Ch 3, turn.

Next Row: Skip first sc, dc into next sc, *3 sc into next ch-5 sp, dc into next sc, dc into next 4-dc cluster, dc into next sc. Repeat from * across, ending row with 3 sc into next ch-5 sp, dec dc to combine last 2 sc. Ch 1, turn.

Next Row: Sc into dec dc, ch 3, *skip next 3 sc, sc into next dc, 4-dc cluster into next dc, sc into next dc, ch 5. Repeat from * across, ending row with skip next 3 sc, sc into next dc, sc into top of turning-ch-3. Ch 3, turn.

Next Row: Skip first sc, dc into next sc, *3 sc into next ch-5 sp, dc into next sc, dc into next 4-dc cluster, dc into next sc. Repeat from * across, ending row with dc into 4-dc cluster, 3-dc dec to combine next sc, ch-3 sp, and last sc. Ch 1, turn.

Next Row: 3-sc dec to combine 3-dc dec and next 2 dc, *ch 5, skip next 3 sc, sc into next dc, 4-dc cluster into next dc, sc into next dc. Repeat from * across, ending row with ch 5, skip next 3 sc, sc into next dc, sc into top of turning-ch-3. Ch 3, turn.

Next Row: Skip first sc, dc into next sc, *3 sc into next ch-5 sp, dc into next sc, dc into next 4-dc cluster, dc into next sc. Repeat from * across, ending row with insert hook under next ch-5 sp and pull up a loop, yarn over hook twice, insert hook into last sc and pull up a loop, (yarn over and draw it through 2 loops on hook) twice, yarn over and draw it through all 3 loops on hook. Fasten off.

❃ Right Front

Work as for left front until piece measures approx 11 (12, 11, 12)"/28 (30.5, 28, 30.5) cm from beg, ending after RS row. *Do not ch 1 to turn.*

Shape Armhole: Next Row (WS): Slip st into first 7 sts, ch 1, sc into same dc as last slip st, sc into next dc, *ch 5, skip next 3 sc, sc into next dc, 4-dc cluster into next dc, sc into next dc. Repeat from * across, ending row with ch 5, skip next 3 sc, sc into next dc, sc into top of turning-ch-3. Ch 3, turn.

Next Row: Skip first sc, dc into next sc, *3 sc into next ch-5 sp, dc into next sc, dc into next 4-dc cluster, dc into next sc. Repeat from * across, end-

ing row with 3 sc into next ch-5 sp, dc into last 2 sc. Ch 1, turn.

Next Row: 3 sc dec to combine the first 2 dc and the next sc, ch 3, *sc into next dc, 4-dc cluster into next dc, sc into next dc, ch 5, skip next 3 sc. Repeat from * across, ending row with sc into last 2 dc. Ch 3, turn.

Next Row: Skip first sc, dc into next sc, *3 sc into next ch-5 sp, dc into next sc, dc into next 4-dc cluster, dc into next sc. Repeat from * across, ending row with 3 sc into next ch-5 sp, dc into next sc, 4-dc dec to combine the next 4-dc cluster, sc, ch-3 sp, and the 3-sc dec. Ch 1, turn.

Cont even in Clusters-and-Lace Patt until piece measures approx 17 (18, 18, 19)"/43 (45.5, 45.5, 48.5) cm from beg, ending after RS row.

Shape Neck: Next Row (WS): Sc into first 2 dc, *ch 5, skip next 3 sc, sc into next dc, 4-dc cluster into next dc, sc into next dc. Repeat from * across until 8 sts rem in row, ending row with sc into next 2 dc. Ch 3, turn, leaving rest of row unworked.

Next Row: Skip 2 sc, *3 sc into next ch-5 sp, dc into next sc, dc into next 4-dc cluster, dc into next sc. Repeat from * across, ending row with 3 sc into next ch-5 sp, dc into last 2 sc. Ch 1, turn.

Next Row: Sc into first 2 dc, *ch 5, skip next 3 sc, sc into next dc, 4-dc cluster into next dc, sc into next dc. Repeat from * across, ending row with ch 3, sc into top of turning-ch. Ch 3, turn.

Next Row: 3-dc dec to combine the ch-3 sp, next sc, and 4-dc cluster, dc into next sc, *3 sc into next ch-5 sp, dc into next sc, dc into next 4-dc cluster, dc into next sc. Repeat from * across, ending row with 3 sc into next ch-5 sp, dc into last 2 sc. Ch 1, turn.

Next Row: Sc into first 2 dc, *ch 5, skip next 3 sc, sc into next dc, 4-dc cluster into next dc, sc into next dc. Repeat from * across, ending row with ch 3, skip next 3 sc, 3-sc dec to combine next sc, 3-dc dec, and the turning-ch. Ch 3, turn.

Next Row: 3-dc dec to combine ch-3 sp, next sc, and 4-dc cluster, dc into next sc, *3 sc into next ch-5 sp, dc into next sc, dc into next 4-dc cluster, dc into next sc. Repeat from * across, ending row with 3 sc into next ch-5 sp, dc into last 2 sc. Fasten off.

❁ Sleeves

With larger hook, ch 50 (50, 56, 56). Beg Clusters-and-Lace Patt, and work even on 49 (49, 55, 55) sts for two rows. Ch 3, turn.

Inc Row 1 (RS): Dc into first sc, dc into next sc, *3 sc into next ch-5 sp, dc into next sc, dc into next 4-dc cluster, dc into next sc. Repeat from * across, ending row with 3 sc into next ch-5 sp, dc into next sc, 2 dc into last sc. Ch 1, turn.

Inc Row 2: Sc into first dc, 4-dc cluster into next dc, sc into next dc, *ch 5, skip next 3 sc, sc into next dc, 4-dc cluster into next dc, sc into next dc. Repeat from * across, ending row with ch 5, skip next 3 sc, sc into next dc, 4-dc cluster into next dc, sc into top of turning-ch-3. Ch 3, turn.

Inc Row 3: Dc into first sc, dc into next 4-dc cluster, dc into next sc, *3 sc into next ch-5 sp, dc into next sc, dc into next 4-dc cluster, dc into next sc. Repeat from * across, ending row with 3 sc into next ch-5 sp, dc into next sc, dc into next 4-dc cluster, 2 dc into last sc. Ch 1, turn.

Inc Row 4: Sc into first 2 dc, *4-dc cluster into next dc, sc into next dc, ch 5, skip next 3 sc, sc into next dc. Repeat from * across, ending row with 4-dc cluster into next dc, sc into next dc, sc into top of turning-ch-3. Ch 3, turn.

Inc Row 5: Dc into first sc, *dc into next sc, dc into next 4-dc cluster, dc into next sc, 3 sc into next ch-5 sp. Repeat from * across, ending row with dc into next sc, dc into next 4-dc cluster, dc into next sc, 2 dc into last sc. Ch 1, turn.

Inc Row 6: Sc into first 3 dc, *4-dc cluster into next dc, sc into next dc, ch 5, skip next 3 sc, sc into next dc. Repeat from * across, ending row with 4-dc cluster into next dc, sc into next 2 dc, sc into top of turning-ch-3. Ch 3, turn.

Inc Row 7: Dc into first 3 sc, *dc into next 4-dc cluster, dc into next sc, 3 sc into next ch-5 sp, dc into next sc. Repeat from * across, ending row with dc into next 4-dc cluster, dc into next 2 sc, 2 dc into last sc. Ch 1, turn.

Inc Row 8: Sc into first dc, ch 5, skip next 2 dc, *sc into next dc, 4-dc cluster into next dc, sc into next dc, ch 5, skip next 3 sc. Repeat from * across, ending row with sc into next dc, 4-dc cluster into next dc, sc into next dc, ch 5, skip next 2 dc, sc into top of turning-ch-3. Ch 3, turn.

Inc Row 9: Dc into first sc, *3 sc into next ch-5 sp, dc into next sc, dc into next 4-dc cluster, dc into next sc. Repeat from * across, ending row with 3 sc into next ch-5 sp, 2 dc into last sc. Ch 1, turn.

Work seven rows even in Clusters-and-Lace Patt. Repeat last sixteen rows once more, then work Inc Rows 1–9 once more.

Cont even until sleeve measures approx 16½"/ 42 cm from beg, ending after RS row. *Do not ch 1 to turn.*

Shape Cap: Next Row (WS): Slip st into first 7 sts, ch 1, sc into same dc as the last slip st, sc into next dc, *ch 5, skip next 3 sc, sc into next dc, 4-dc cluster into next dc, sc into next dc. Repeat from * across until 7 sts rem in row, ending row with sc into next st. Ch 3, turn, leaving rest of row unworked.

Next Row: Skip first sc, dc into next dc, *3 sc into next ch-5 sp, dc into next sc, dc into next 4-dc cluster, dc into next sc. Repeat from * across, ending row with 3 sc into next ch-5 sp, dc into last 2 sc. Ch 1, turn.

Next Row: 3-sc dec to combine the first 2 dc and the next sc, ch 3, *sc into next dc, 4-dc cluster into next dc, sc into next dc, ch 5, skip next 3 sc. Repeat from * across, ending row with sc into next dc, 4-dc cluster into next dc, sc into next dc, ch 3, skip next 2 sc, 3-sc dec to combine the next sc, the next dc, and the turning-ch-3. Ch 3, turn.

Next Row: 3-dc dec to combine the ch-3 sp, the next sc, and the next 4-dc cluster, dc into next sc, *3 sc into next ch-5 sp, dc into next sc, dc into next 4-dc cluster, dc into next sc. Repeat from * across, ending row with 3 sc into next ch-5 sp, dc into next sc, 4-dc dec to combine the next 4-dc cluster, the next sc, the next ch-3 sp, and the 3-sc dec. Ch 1, turn.

Next Row: Sc into 4-dc dec and into next dc, *ch 5, skip next 3 sc, sc into next dc, 4-dc cluster into next dc, sc into next dc. Repeat from * across, ending row with ch 5, skip next 3 sc, dec sc to combine next 2 dc, sc into top of turning-ch-3. Ch 3, turn.

Next Row: Skip first sc, dc into next dc, *3 sc into next ch-5 sp, dc into next sc, dc into next 4-dc cluster, dc into next sc. Repeat from * across, ending row with 3 sc into next ch-5 sp, dc into last 2 sc. Ch 1, turn.

Next Row: 3-sc dec to combine the first 2 dc and the next sc, ch 3, *sc into next dc, 4-dc cluster into next dc, sc into next dc, ch 5, skip next 3 sc. Repeat from * across, ending row with sc into next dc, 4-dc cluster into next dc, sc into next dc, ch 3, skip next 3 sc, 3-sc dec to combine the next sc, the next dc, and the turning-ch-3. Ch 3, turn.

Next Row: 3-dc dec to combine the ch-3 sp, the next sc, and the next 4-dc cluster, dc into next sc, *3 sc into next ch-5 sp, dc into next sc, dc into next 4-dc cluster, dc into next sc. Repeat from * across, ending row with 3 sc into next ch-5 sp, dc into next sc, 4-dc dec to combine the next 4-dc cluster, the next sc, the next ch-3 sp, and the 3-sc dec. Ch 1, turn.

Next Row: 3-sc dec to combine the dc dec, the next dc, and the next sc, ch 3, *sc into next dc, 4-dc cluster into next dc, sc into next dc, ch 5, skip next 3 sc. Repeat from * across, ending row with sc into next dc, 4-dc cluster into next dc, sc into next dc, ch 3, skip next 3 sc, 3-sc dec to combine the next dc, the next dec dc, and the turning-ch-3. Ch 3, turn.

Next Row: 3-dc dec to combine the ch-3 sp, the next sc, and the next 4-dc cluster, dc into next sc, *3 sc into next ch-5 sp, dc into next sc, dc into next 4-dc cluster, dc into next sc. Repeat from * across, ending row with 3 sc into next ch-5 sp, dc into next sc, 4-dc dec to combine the next 4-dc cluster, the next sc, the next ch-3 sp, and the 3-sc dec. Ch 1, turn.

Next Row: Sc into first 4-dc dec, sc into next dc, *ch 5, skip next 3 sc, sc into next dc, 4-dc cluster into next dc, sc into next dc. Repeat from * across, ending row with ch 5, skip next 3 sc, sc into next dc, dec sc to combine 3-dc dec and top of turning-ch-3. Ch 3, turn.

Next Row: Skip first sc, dc into next dc, *3 sc into next ch-5 sp, dc into next sc, dc into next 4-dc

cluster, dc into next sc. Repeat from * across, ending row with 3 sc into next ch-5 sp, dc into last 2 sc. Ch 1, turn.

Next Row: 3-sc dec to combine the first 2 dc and the next sc, ch 3, *sc into next dc, 4-dc cluster into next dc, sc into next dc, ch 5, skip next 3 sc. Repeat from * across, ending row with sc into next dc, 4-dc cluster into next dc, sc into next dc, ch 3, skip next 2 sc, 3-sc dec to combine the next sc, the next dc, and the turning-ch-3. Ch 3, turn.

Next Row: 3-dc dec to combine the ch-3 sp, the next sc, and the next 4-dc cluster, dc into next sc, *3 sc into next ch-5 sp, dc into next sc, dc into next 4-dc cluster, dc into next sc. Repeat from * across, ending row with 3 sc into next ch-5 sp, dc into next sc, 4-dc dec to combine the next 4-dc cluster, the next sc, the next ch-3 sp, and the 3-sc dec. Ch 1, turn.

Sc into first 4-dc dec, sc into next dc, *ch 5, skip next 3 sc, sc into next dc, 4-dc cluster into next dc, sc into next dc. Repeat from * across, ending row with ch 5, skip next 3 sc, sc into next dc, dec sc to combine 3-dc dec and top of turning-ch-3. Ch 3, turn.

Next Row: Skip first sc, dc into next dc, *3 sc into next ch-5 sp, dc into next sc, dc into next 4-dc cluster, dc into next sc. Repeat from * across, ending row with 3 sc into next ch-5 sp, dc into last 2 sc. Fasten off.

✿ Finishing

Back Lower Edging: With RS facing and smaller hook, attach yarn with a slip st to first ch of foundation ch on back, and ch 1.

Row 1 (RS): Working into unworked loops of foundation ch, work sc into each ch across. Ch 3, turn.

Row 2: Dc into first sc, *skip next 2 sc, (dc, ch 1, dc) into next sc. Repeat from * across, ending row with skip next 2 sc, 2 dc into last sc. Ch 1, turn.

Row 3: Sc into first dc, *[3 dc, ch 3, slip st into third ch from hook (*picot made*), 3 dc] into next ch-1 sp, sc into next ch-1 sp. Repeat from * across, ending row with (3 dc, picot, 3 dc) into next ch-1 sp, sc into top of turning-ch-3. Fasten off.

Left Front, Right Front, and Sleeve Bottom Edging: Work as for back lower edging.

Sew shoulder seams.

Buttonband: With RS facing and smaller hook, attach yarn with a slip st to beg of neck shaping on left front, and ch 1. Work 91 (95, 95, 99) sc along left front edge. Ch 1, turn.

Cont even in sc until band measures approx 1½"/ 4 cm from beg. Fasten off.

Place markers for seven evenly spaced buttons along band, making the first and last ½"/1.5 cm from lower edge and beg of neck shaping.

Buttonhole Band: With RS facing and smaller hook, attach yarn with a slip st to lower right front edge and ch 1. Work 91 (95, 95, 99) sc along right front edge. Ch 1, turn.

Cont even in sc until band measures approx ¾"/ 2 cm from beg.

Next Row: Cont in sc, making seven buttonholes by working (ch 4, skip 4 sc) opposite markers.

Next Row: Cont in sc, working 4 sc into each ch-4 sp of previous row.

Cont even in sc until band measures approx 1½"/ 4 cm from beg. Fasten off.

Collar: With smaller hook and RS facing, work 79 sc around neckline, beg and end halfway into front bands. Ch 1, turn.

Row 1: Sc into each sc across. Ch 3, turn.

Row 2: Dc into first sc, *skip next 2 sc, (dc, ch 1, dc) into next sc. Repeat from * across, ending row with skip next 2 sc, 2 dc into last sc. Ch 4, turn.

Row 3: Dc into first dc, *(dc, ch 1, dc) into next ch-1 sp. Repeat from * across, ending row with (dc, ch 1, dc) into top of turning-ch-3. Ch 3, turn.

Row 4: *(Dc, ch 1, dc) into next ch-1 sp. Repeat from * across, ending row with (dc, ch 1, dc) under turning-ch-4, dc into third ch of turning-ch-4. Ch 4, turn.

Repeat Rows 3 and 4 twice more. Fasten off.

Collar Edging: With RS of collar facing, attach yarn with a slip st to first row of collar on left front. Sc into same st as slip st, skip first (dc, ch 1, dc) row, *into next row work (3 dc, picot, 3 dc), sc into next row. Repeat from * evenly along side edge of collar twice more, ending with sc into first dc of eighth row of collar. Working along edge of collar, **(3 dc, picot, 3 dc) into next ch-1 sp, sc into next ch-1 sp. Repeat from ** across, ending row with (3 dc, picot, 3 dc) into next ch-1 sp, sc into top of turning-ch-3. Working along right side edge of collar, ***(3 dc, picot, 3 dc), sc. Repeat from *** evenly along right side edge of collar twice more, ending with sc into first row of collar. Fasten off.

Set in sleeves. Sew sleeve and side seams. Sew on buttons.

Autumn Pullover

Cozy up into fall with this fashion-forward raglan sweater. Its spicy colors will keep you warm inside and out.

❖ Sizes

Small (Medium, Large, Extra-Large). Instructions are for smallest size, with changes for other sizes noted in parentheses as necessary.

❖ Finished Measurements

Bust: 38½ (41½, 44½, 47½)"/98 (105.5, 113, 120.5) cm
Length: 27¾ (28¼, 29½, 30)"/70.5 (72, 75, 76) cm
Sleeve width at upper arm: 14¾ (15¾, 16¼, 16¾)"/37.5 (40, 41.5, 42.5) cm

❖ Materials

Coats and Clark's *Red Heart Soft* (heavy worsted weight; 100% acrylic with Bounce-Back® fibers; 5 oz/140 g; approx 328 yd/300 m), 3 (3, 4, 4) skeins Rust #7285 (A), 3 (3, 3, 4) skeins Gold #7322 (B), and 2 (3, 3, 4) skeins Dark Yellow Green #7675 (C).
Crochet hook, size H/8 (5.00 mm) or size needed to obtain gauge.

❖ Gauge

In Long Bobble Patt, 16 sts and 12 rows = 4"/10 cm.
To measure your gauge, make a test swatch as follows: Ch 18. Work Long Bobble Patt for 12 rows. Fasten off.
Piece should measure 4¼"/11 cm wide and 4"/10 cm long. **To save time, take time to check gauge.**

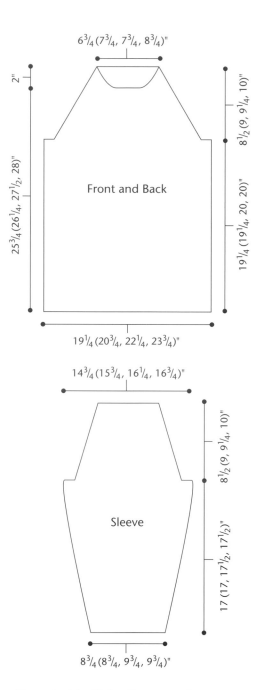

Pattern Notes:

- Long Bobble = Yarn over, insert hook around the post of next dc *from front to back to front* and pull up a loop, yarn over and draw it through 2 loops on hook, (yarn over, insert hook from front to back to front around post of same dc and pull up a loop, yarn over and draw it through 2 loops on hook) three times, yarn over and draw it through all 5 loops on hook.
- Each turning-ch-3 counts as 1 dc.
- To decrease in dc, work until 2 sts rem in row, then work a dec dc to combine the last 2 sts in row. On the next row, work last st into the last dc, not into the top of the turning-ch-3.
- To decrease in sc, work a dec sc to combine the first 2 sts and the last 2 sts of the row.
- To increase, work 2 sts into a st.
- To change color, work until 2 loops rem on hook; with second color, complete the st; fasten off first color.
- For a description and illustration of any unfamiliar stitch, refer to the back of the book.

❀ Long Bobble Patt

With A, ch multiple of 6

Foundation Row (RS): Sc into second ch from hook and into each ch across. Ch 3, turn.

Rows 1 and All WS Rows: Skip first sc, dc into each st across. Change color, ch 1, turn.

Row 2: Sc into first 5 dc, *Long Bobble into next dc, skip dc behind Long Bobble just made, sc into next 5 dc. Repeat from * across, ending row with Long Bobble into next dc, skip dc behind Long Bobble just made, sc into next 4 dc, sc into top of turning-ch-3. Ch 3, turn.

Row 4: Sc into first 2 dc, *Long Bobble into next dc, skip dc behind Long Bobble just made, sc into next 5 dc. Repeat from * across, ending row with Long Bobble into next st, skip dc behind Long Bobble just made, sc into next dc, sc into top of turning-ch-3. Ch 3, turn.

Repeat Rows 1–4 in Color Sequence for patt.

❀ Sideways Rib Patt

Over any number of ch

Foundation Row: Sc into second ch from hook and into each ch across. Ch 1, turn.

Patt Row: Sc *into the back loop* of each sc across. Ch 1, turn.

Repeat Patt Row.

❁ Color Sequence

2 rows A

2 rows B

2 rows C

Repeat for patt.

❁ Back

With A, ch 78 (84, 90, 96). Work Long Bobble Patt in Color Sequence until piece measures approx 19¼ (19¼, 20, 20)"/49 (49, 51, 51) cm from beg, ending after WS row—77 (83, 89, 95) sts each row. Fasten off.

Shape Raglan Armhole: With RS facing, skip first 4 sts and attach next color with a slip st to next st and ch 1. Cont in patt across next 69 (75, 81, 87) sts, ch 3, turn, leaving last 4 sts unworked.

Cont in patt as established, dec 1 st each side every other row 4 (4, 2, 3) times, then every row 17 (18, 23, 23) times—27 (31, 31, 35) sts rem. Fasten off.

❁ Front

Work as for back until 39 (43, 43, 47) sts rem.

Shape Neck: Next Row (RS): Make raglan dec st at armhole edge, work patt as established across next 8 sts, work dec st, turn, leaving last 27 (31, 31, 35) unworked.

Cont patt as established, working raglan decs same as for back; **at the same time,** dec 1 st at neck edge every row. Fasten off.

For second side of neck, with RS facing, skip the middle 15 (19, 19, 23) sts, attach yarn with a slip st to next st and complete as for first side of neck.

❁ Sleeves

With A, ch 9. Work Sideways Rib Patt until piece measures approx 8½ (8½, 9½, 9½)"/21.5 (21.5, 24, 24) cm from beg—8 sc each row. Ch 1, turn.

Sleeve Foundation Row (RS): Work 35 (35, 39, 39) sc evenly across long side of ribbing. Ch 3, turn.

Skip Foundation Row of Long Bobble Patt. Beg with Row 1 of patt, and work Long Bobble Patt in Color Sequence, and inc 1 st each side every other row 3 (7, 4, 6) times, then every fourth row 9 (7, 9, 8) times—59 (63, 65, 67) sts. Cont even until sleeve measures 17 (17, 17½, 17½)"/43 (43, 44.5, 44.5) cm from beg, ending after WS row. Fasten off.

Shape Raglan Armholes: With RS facing, skip first 4 sts and attach next color with a slip st to next st and ch 1. Cont in patt across next 51 (55, 57, 59) sts, ch 3, turn, leaving last 4 sts unworked.

Cont in patt as established, dec 1 st each side every other row 6 (5, 6, 7) times, then every row 13 (16, 15, 15) times   13 (13, 15, 15) sts rem. Fasten off.

❁ Finishing

Sew raglan seams.

Sew sleeve and side seams.

Neckband: With RS facing and A, work 87 (95, 95, 101) sc around neckline. Fasten off.

With A, ch 20. Work Sideways Rib Patt until piece, when slightly stretched, fits around neckline—19 sc each row. Fasten off.

Sew foundation row of neckband to the last row of the neckband. Sewing *through back loops* of each sc, sew neck ribbing into place in neckline, placing seam at center of back neck.

Ida's Springtime Cardigan

The delicate front border and subtle texture of this sweater are highlighted with a row of beautiful carved buttons. The functional besom pockets will make this a wardrobe favorite.

INTERMEDIATE

❖ Sizes

Small (Medium, Large, Extra-Large). Instructions are for smallest size, with changes for other sizes noted in parentheses as necessary.

❖ Finished Measurements

Bust (Buttoned): 39 (42¾, 46¼, 50)"/99 (108.5, 117.5, 127) cm
Length (Including Edging): 21½ (22½, 22½, 23½)"/54.5 (57, 57, 59.5) cm
Sleeve width at upper arm: 18 (18, 20, 20)"/45.5 (45.5, 51, 51) cm

❖ Materials

Coats and Clark's *Lustersheen* (fingering weight; 100% acrylic; 1⅘ oz/51.5 g; approx 150 yd/135 m), 17 (18, 19, 20) balls Tea Leaf #615
Crochet hooks, sizes D/3 and E/4 (3.25 and 3.50 mm) or size needed to obtain gauge
Ten ½"/13 mm buttons (One World Button Supply Company's *Flower Shirt Button Style #NPL 223-13* was used on sample garment)

❖ Gauge

In patt with larger hook, each 5-dc shell measures ¾"/2 cm wide.
To measure your gauge, make a test swatch as follows: With larger hook, ch 28. Work Ida's Textured Patt for nine rows. Fasten off.
Piece should measure 3¾"/9.5 cm wide and 3"/7.5 cm long. **To save time, take time to check gauge.**

Pattern Notes:

- Each turning-ch-3 counts as a dc.
- 5=dc shell = dc into indicated st.
- For a description and illustration of any un-familiar stitch, refer to the back of the book.

❧ Ida's Textured Patt

Ch multiple of 6 + 4

Foundation Row (RS): 2 dc into fourth ch from hook, *skip next 2 ch, dc into next ch, skip next 2 ch, 5 dc into next ch. Repeat from * across, ending row with skip next 2 ch, dc into next ch, skip next 2 ch, 3 dc into last ch. Ch 3, turn.

Row 1 (WS): Skip first 3 dc, *5 dc into next dc, skip next 2 dc, dc into next dc, skip next 2 dc. Repeat from * across, ending row with 5 dc into next dc, skip next 2 dc, dc into top of turning-ch-3. Ch 3, turn.

Row 2: 2 dc into first dc, *skip next 2 dc, dc into next dc, skip next 2 dc, 5 dc into next dc. Repeat from * across, ending row with skip next 2 dc, dc into next dc, skip next 2 dc, 3 dc into top of turning-ch-3. Ch 3, turn.

Repeat Rows 1 and 2 for patt.

❧ Back

With larger hook, ch 130 (142, 154, 166). Beg Ida's Textured Patt, and work even on 127 (139, 151, 163) sts until piece measures approx 12 (13, 12, 13)"/30.5 (33, 30.5, 33) cm from beg, ending after WS row. *Do not ch 3 to turn.*

Shape Armholes: Next Row (RS): Slip st into first 13 (19, 19, 25) sts, ch 3, 2 dc into same dc as last slip st, (skip next 2 dc, dc into next dc, skip next 2 dc, 5 dc into next dc) 16 (16, 18, 18) times, skip next 2 dc, dc into next dc, skip next 2 dc, 3 dc

into next dc, ch 3, turn, leaving rest of row unworked.

Cont even on these 103 (103, 115, 115) sts until armholes measure approx 8 (8, 9, 9)"/20.5 (20.5, 23, 23) cm, ending after WS row. Ch 3, turn.

Shape Neck: Next Row (RS): 2 dc into first dc, (skip next 2 dc, dc into next dc, skip next 2 dc, 5 dc into next dc) 4 (4, 5, 5) times, skip next 2 dc, dc into next dc, skip next 2 dc, 3 dc into next dc, ch 3, turn, leaving rest of row unworked—31 (31, 37, 37) sts rem.

Cont even on this side until armhole measures 9 (9, 10, 10)"/23 (23, 25.5, 25.5) cm. Fasten off.

For second side of neck, with RS facing and larger hook, skip the middle 41 sts and attach yarn with a slip st to next st and ch 3. Complete as for first side.

❧ Pocket Linings (Make Two)

With larger hook, ch 34. Beg Ida's Textured Patt, and work even on 31 sts for fourteen rows total. Fasten off.

❧ Left Front

With larger hook, ch 64 (70, 76, 82). Beg Ida's Textured Patt, and work even on 61 (67, 73, 79) sts until piece measures approx 5¼"/13.5 cm from beg, ending after WS row. Ch 3, turn.

Place Pocket Lining: Next Row (RS): 2 dc into first dc, (skip next 2 dc, dc into next dc, skip next 2 dc, 5 dc into next dc) 1 (2, 2, 3) times, skip next 2 dc, dc into next dc, skip next 2 dc, then, with RS of pocket lining facing, work across 31 sts from lining, work to end row.

Cont even until piece measures approx 12 (13, 12, 13)"/30.5 (33, 30.5, 33) cm from beg, ending after WS row. *Do not ch 3 to turn.*

Shape Armhole: Next Row (RS): Slip st across first 13 (19, 19, 25) sts, ch 3, work in patt to end row.

Cont even on 49 (49, 55, 55) sts until piece measures approx 14¼ (15¼, 15¼, 16¼)"/36 (38.5, 38.5, 41.5) cm from beg, ending after WS row. Ch 3, turn.

Shape Neck: Neck Dec Row 1: (RS): 2 dc into first dc, *skip next 2 dc, dc into next dc, skip next 2 dc, 5 dc into next dc. Repeat from * across, ending row with skip next 2 dc, yarn over, insert hook into next dc and pull up a loop, yarn over and draw it through 2 loops, yarn over, skip next 2 dc, insert hook into top of turning-ch-3 and pull up a loop, yarn over and draw it through 2 loops, yarn over and draw it through all 3 loops on hook. Ch 3, turn.

Neck Dec Row 2: 2 dc into first st, *skip next 2 dc, dc into next dc, skip next 2 dc, 5 dc into next dc. Repeat from * across, ending row with skip next 2 dc, dc into top of turning-ch-3. Ch 3, turn.

Neck Dec Row 3: Work same as Neck Dec Row 2. Ch 3, turn.

Neck Dec Row 4: Skip first 3 dc, dc into next dc, *skip next 2 dc, 5 dc into next dc, skip next 2 dc, dc into next dc. Repeat from * across, ending row with skip next 2 dc, 5 dc into next dc, skip next 2 dc, dc into top of turning-ch-3. Ch 3, turn.

Neck Dec Row 5: 2 dc into first dc, *skip next 2 dc, dc into next dc, skip next 2 dc, 5 dc into next dc. Repeat from * across, ending row with skip next 2 dc, dc into next dc, skip next 3 dc, 3 dc into top of turning-ch-3. Ch 3, turn.

Neck Dec Row 6: Skip next 3 dc, *5 dc into next dc, skip next 2 dc, dc into next dc, skip next 2 dc. Repeat from * across, ending row with 5 dc into next dc, skip next 2 dc, dc into top of turning-ch-3. Ch 3, turn.

Repeat Neck Dec Rows 1–6 twice more—31 (31, 37, 37) sts rem.

Cont even until piece measures same as back. Fasten off.

❀ Right Front

Work same as left front until piece measures approx 5¼"/13.5 cm from beg, ending after WS row. Ch 3, turn.

Place Pocket Lining: Next Row (RS): 2 dc into first dc, (skip next 2 dc, dc into next dc, skip next 2 dc, 5 dc into next dc) 2 (2, 3, 3) times, skip next 2 dc, dc into next dc, skip next 2 dc, then, with RS of pocket lining facing, work across 31 sts from lining, work to end row.

Cont even until piece measures approx 12 (13, 12, 13)"/30.5 (33, 30.5, 33) cm from beg, ending after WS row.

Shape Armhole: Next Row (RS): Work across first 49 (49, 55, 55) sts, ch 3, turn, leaving last 12 (18, 18, 24) sts unworked.

Cont even until piece measures approx 14¼ (15¼, 15¼, 16¼)"/36 (38.5, 38.5, 41.5) cm from beg, ending after WS row. Ch 3, turn.

Shape Neck: Neck Dec Row 1: (RS): Skip first 3 dc, *dc into next dc, skip next 2 dc, 5 dc into next dc, skip next 2 dc. Repeat from * across,

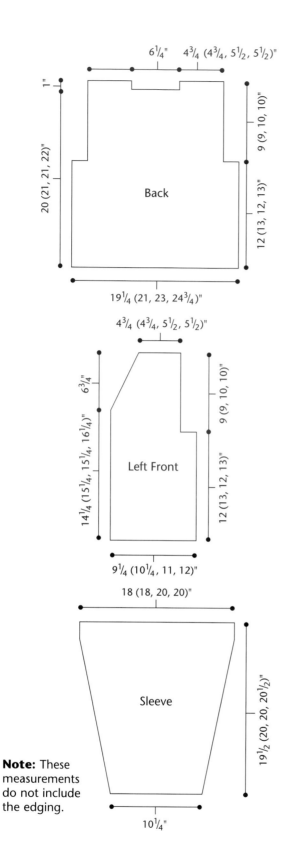

Back

6¼" 4¾" (4¾", 5½", 5½")"

1"

20 (21, 21, 22)"

9 (9, 10, 10)"

12 (13, 12, 13)"

19¼ (21, 23, 24¾)"

Left Front

4¾" (4¾", 5½", 5½")"

6¾"

14¼ (15¼, 15¼, 16¼)"

9 (9, 10, 10)"

12 (13, 12, 13)"

9¼ (10¼, 11, 12)"

Sleeve

18 (18, 20, 20)"

19½ (20, 20, 20½)"

10¼"

Note: These measurements do not include the edging.

ending row with 3 dc into top of turning-ch-3. Ch 3, turn.

Neck Dec Row 2: Skip first 3 dc, *5 dc into next dc, skip next 2 dc, dc into next dc, skip next 2 dc.

Repeat from * across, ending row with skip next 3 dc, 3 dc into top of turning-ch-3. Ch 3, turn.

Neck Dec Row 3: Skip first 3 dc, *5 dc into next dc, skip next 2 dc, dc into next dc, skip next 2 dc. Repeat from * across, ending row with skip next 2 dc, 3 dc into top of turning-ch-3. Ch 3, turn.

Neck Dec Row 4: Skip first 3 dc, *5 dc into next dc, skip next 2 dc, dc into next dc, skip next 2 dc. Repeat from * across, ending row with 5 dc into next dc, skip next 2 dc, yarn over, insert hook into next dc and pull up a loop, yarn over and draw it through 2 loops, skip next 2 dc, yarn over, insert hook into top of turning-ch-3 and pull up a loop, yarn over and draw it through 2 loops, yarn over and draw it through all 3 loops on hook. Ch 3, turn.

Neck Dec Row 5: 2 dc into first dc, * skip next 2 dc, dc into next dc, skip next 2 dc, 5 dc into next dc. Repeat from * across, ending row with skip next 2 dc, dc into next dc, skip next 2 dc, 3 dc into top of turning-ch-3. Ch 3, turn.

Neck Dec Row 6: Skip first 3 dc, *5 dc into next dc, skip next 2 dc, dc into next dc, skip next 2 dc. Repeat from * across, ending row with 5 dc into next dc, skip next 2 dc, dc into top of turning-ch-3. Ch 3, turn.

Repeat Neck Dec Rows 1–6 twice more—31 (31, 37, 37) sts rem.

Complete as for left front.

❈ Sleeves

With larger hook, ch 70. Beg Ida's Textured Patt, working even on 67 sts for two rows total. Ch 3, turn.

Inc Row 1: 4 dc into first dc, *skip next 2 dc, dc into next dc, skip next 2 dc, 5 dc into next dc. Repeat from * across, ending row with skip next 2 dc, dc into next dc, skip next 2 dc, 5 dc into top of turning-ch-3. Ch 3, turn.

When making your foundation chain, always leave a long tail at the beginning. If you use it for seaming your garment, you will have fewer yarn tails to hide.

Inc Row 2: Skip first 2 dc, *dc into next dc, skip next 2 dc, 5 dc into next dc, skip next 2 dc. Repeat from * across, ending row with dc into next dc, skip next dc, dc into top of turning-ch-3. Ch 3, turn.

Inc Row 3: Skip first dc, *5 dc into next dc, skip next 2 dc, dc into next dc, skip next 2 dc. Repeat from * across, ending row with 5 dc into next dc, dc into top of turning-ch-3. Ch 3, turn.

Inc Row 4: 2 dc into first dc, *skip next 2 dc, dc into next dc, skip next 2 dc, 5 dc into next dc. Repeat from * across, ending row with skip next 2 dc, dc into next dc, skip next 2 dc, 3 dc into top of turning-ch-3. Ch 3, turn.

Inc Row 5: Skip first 3 dc, *5 dc into next dc, skip next 2 dc, dc into next dc, skip next 2 dc. Repeat from * across, ending row with 5 dc into next dc, skip next 2 dc, dc into top of turning-ch-3. Ch 3, turn.

Repeat Inc Rows 1–5 for a total of 8 (8, 10, 10) more times—121 (121, 133, 133) sts.

Work even until sleeve measures approx 19½ (20, 20, 20½)"/49.5 (51, 51, 52) cm from beg. Fasten off.

❀ Finishing

Sew shoulder seams. Set in sleeves. Sew sleeve and side seams.

Lower Edging: With RS facing and smaller hook, attach yarn with a slip st to lower left front edge and ch 1. Work three rows sc along entire bottom edge. Fasten off.

Front Bands: With RS facing and smaller hook, attach yarn with a slip st to right front edge and ch 1.

Row 1 (RS): Work 311 (335, 353, 377) sc along right front, across back of neck, and down left front. Ch 1, turn.

Row 2: Sc into each sc, working dec sc each side at beg back neck shaping—309 (333, 351, 375) sc. Ch 1, turn.

Row 3: Work as for last row—307 (331, 349, 373) sc. Ch 1, turn.

Rows 4 and 5: Work even in sc. Ch 1, turn. After Row 5, ch 5 to turn instead of ch 1.

Row 6 (WS): Skip first 3 sc, *dc into next sc, ch 2, skip next 2 sc. Repeat from * across, ending row with dc into last sc. Ch 1, turn.

Row 7: Skip first dc, *(sc, 2 dc, sc) into next ch-2 sp. Repeat from * across, ending row with slip st into third ch of turning ch 5. Fasten off.

Sleeve Edging: With RS facing and smaller hook, attach yarn with a slip st to sleeve seam and ch 1.

Rnd 1: Work 67 sc around lower edge of sleeve.

Complete same as front bands.

Sew sides of sleeve edging tog.

Pocket Edgings: With RS facing and smaller hook, work three rows of sc along top of pockets. Fasten off.

Sew pocket linings into place on WS. Sew sides of pocket edgings to RS of fronts.

Place markers for ten evenly spaced buttons along left front edge, placing them directly opposite ch-2 buttonhole spaces. Sew on buttons.

❧ Basic Stitches and Variations

❧ *Basic Stitches*

Chain (ch)

Begin by making a slip knot on your hook. Wrap the yarn around the hook and draw it through the loop on the hook to form the first chain. Repeat this step as many times as instructed. In patterns, the loop on the hook is never included when counting the number of chain stitches.

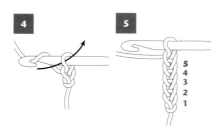

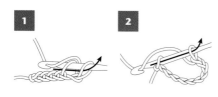

Slip Stitch

Insert hook into the indicated stitch, yarn over; draw it through both the stitch and the loop on the hook (1). Often, slip stitch is used to form a ring. To do so, make a foundation chain as specified in the instructions, and then work a slip stitch into the first chain made (2).

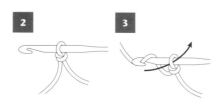

Single Crochet (sc)

Insert hook into indicated stitch, yarn over and pull up a loop; yarn over and draw it through both loops on hook.

Half Double Crochet (hdc)

Yarn over, insert hook into indicated stitch, yarn over and pull up a loop; yarn over and draw it through all three loops on hook.

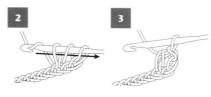

Double Crochet (dc)

Yarn over, insert hook into indicated stitch, yarn over and pull up a loop; (yarn over and draw it through two loops on hook) twice.

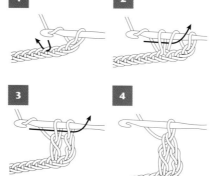

Triple Crochet (tr)

Yarn over hook twice, insert hook into indicated stitch, yarn over and pull up a loop; (yarn over and draw it through two loops on hook) three times.

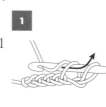

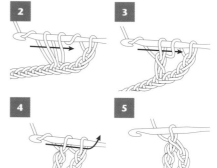

Double Triple Crochet (dtr)

Yarn over hook three times, insert hook into indicated stitch and pull up a loop; (yarn over and draw it through two loops on hook) four times.

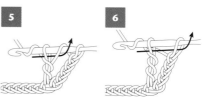

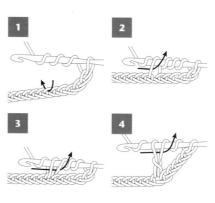

Long Double Crochet (long dc)

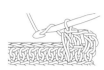

Elongated double crochet worked into the next stitch two rows below.

Front Post Double Crochet (FPDC)

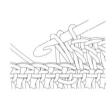

Yarn over hook, insert hook from front to back around the post of indicated stitch, yarn over and pull up a loop; (yarn over and draw it through two loops on hook) twice. Unless noted otherwise, always skip the stitch behind the FPDC.

Back Post Double Crochet (BPDC)

Yarn over hook, insert hook from back to front around the post of indicated stitch, yarn over and pull up a loop; (yarn over and draw it through two loops on hook) twice. Unless noted otherwise, always skip the stitch behind the BPDC.

Front Post Triple Crochet (FPTR)

Yarn over hook twice, insert hook from front to back around the post of indicated stitch, yarn over and pull up a loop; (yarn over and draw it through two loops on hook) three times. Unless noted otherwise, always skip the stitch behind the FPTR.

Back Post Triple Crochet (BPTR)

Yarn over hook twice, insert hook from back to front around the post of indicated stitch, yarn over and draw it through

two loops on hook) three times. Unless noted otherwise, always skip the stitch behind the BPTR.

Front Post Double Triple Crochet (FPDTR)

Yarn over hook three times, insert hook from front to back around the post of indicated stitch, yarn over and pull up a loop; (yarn over and draw it through two loops on hook) four times. Unless noted otherwise, always skip the stitch behind the FPDTR.

Decrease Single Crochet (dec sc)

(Insert hook into next stitch and draw up a loop) twice, yarn over and draw it through all three loops on hook.

Decrease Half Double Crochet (dec hdc)

(Yarn over, insert hook into next stitch and pull up a loop, yarn over) twice, yarn over and draw it through all five loops on hook.

Decrease Double Crochet (dec dc)

(Yarn over, insert hook into next stitch, yarn over and pull up a loop,

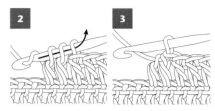

yarn over and draw it through two loops on hook) twice, yarn over and draw it through all three loops on hook.

Bobble

Five double crochet stitches into next stitch, drop loop from hook; insert hook from front to back into

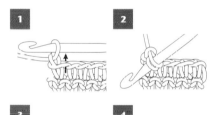

the first double crochet stitch made, replace loop onto hook and draw loop through.

Reverse Single Crochet (reverse sc)

Working from left to right, insert hook into next stitch, yarn over and pull up a loop; yarn over and draw it through both loops on hook.

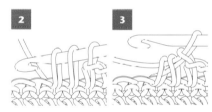

Working into the back loop only

Instead of working into both loops of the indicated stitch, insert the hook under the back loop only.

❀ Seaming

After investing time and effort to cro-chet the pieces of a garment, be sure to put the same amount of care and attention into assembling it.

❀ *Verticle Seams*

For invisible vertical seams (such as side and sleeve seams), use the mat-tress stitch, as follows.

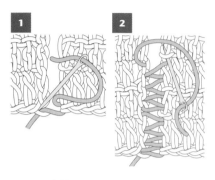

1. *Carefully pin the two pieces together, matching patterns and stripes.*

2. *Thread a tapestry needle with your yarn. Bring the needle up from back to front through the lower right-hand corner of the left-hand piece of fabric, leaving a 6"/15 cm tail.*

3. *Bring the yarn up and through the bottom edge of the first stitch on the right-hand piece to secure the lower edges.*

4. *Bring the yarn up and through the first stitch on the left-hand piece from front to back to front. It is usu-ally best to actually go under strands in the center of the stitch to form a sturdy seam.*

5. *Insert the needle into the correspond-ing place on the right-hand piece from front to back to front.*

6. *Repeat the last two steps.*

7. *After you have joined four rows or so, pull tautly on the seaming yarn, allowing one half of each edge stitch to roll to the wrong side to form a seam.*

8. *Repeat the last two steps, catching the side stitches of each piece until the seam is completed.*

9. *Weave in tails on the wrong side of the work.*

❀ Abbreviations

approx	approximately	patt(s)	pattern(s)
beg	begin(ning)	rem	remain(ing)
BPDC	back post double crochet	rnd(s)	round(s)
		RH	right-hand
BPTR	back post triple crochet	RS	right side
		sc	single crochet
ch(s)	chain(s)	sp(s)	space(s)
ch-sp	chain space	st(s)	stitch(es)
cm	centimeter(s)	tog	together
cont	continu(e)(ing)	tr	triple crochet
dc	double crochet	WS	wrong side
dec	decreas(e)(ing)	yd	yard(s)
dtr	double triple crochet	*, **, ***	repeat instructions after asterisk(s) or between asterisks across row or for as many times as instructed
FPDC	front post double cro-chet		
FPDTR	front post double triple crochet		
FPTR	front post triple crochet	( ), [ ]	repeat instructions within parentheses (and/or brackets) for as many times as instructed
hdc	half double crochet		
inc	increas(e)(ing)		
LH	left-hand		
mm	millimeter(s)		
oz	ounce(s)		

❀ UK Equivalents

American Term	UK Term
Double crochet (dc)	Treble (tr)
Double triple crochet (dtr)	Triple treble (tr tr)
Gauge	Tension
Half double crochet (hdc)	Half treble (htr)
Single crochet (sc)	double crochet (dc)
Slip stitch	Single crochet (sc)
Triple crochet (tr)	Double treble crochet (dtr)
Yarn over	Yarn over hook (yoh)

❧ Horizontal Seams

For invisible horizontal seams (such as shoulder seams), work the same as vertical seams, except insert the tapestry needle into the top of the stitches on the last row of the two pieces you are seaming.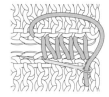

❧ Sweater Assembly

In basic drop-shoulder garments, the shoulders are typically seamed together first, then the sleeves are attached to the body of the garment, and finally the sleeve and side seams are joined.

Sweaters with indented armholes, however, require a little more attention when seaming the underarm area. Refer to the drawings below when assembling pullovers or cardigans with armhole shaping.

❧ Yarns

Each sweater in this book was designed for a particular yarn. Because of unique characteristics such as fiber content, twist, texture, and other qualities, each yarn behaves differently when crocheted into a fabric. For the best results, I recommend that you use the suggested yarn for each project.

If, however, you would like to make a yarn substitution, be sure to choose one of similar weight to the one called for in the pattern. Work up a swatch of solid single crochet in the yarn you prefer and count the number of stitches over 4"/10 cm to determine its weight.

Yarn Weight	Stitches per 4"/10 cm
Fingering weight	24 or more
Sport weight	22–24
Light worsted weight	20–22
Worsted weight	19–20
Heavy worsted weight	16–18
Bulky weight	15 or fewer

Basic Drop Shoulder

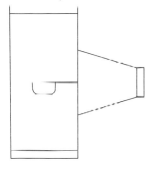

Square Indented Armhole

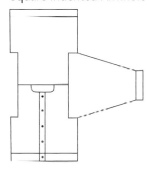

Set-In Sleeve

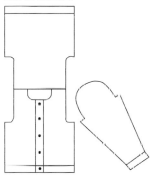

Angled Indented Armhole

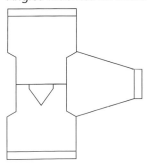

Saddle Shoulder

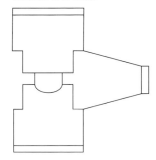

✤ Resources

✤ Manufacturers

These companies sell wholesale only. Contact them to locate retail stores in your area.

Bernat Yarns
See Spinrite, Inc.

Berroco, Inc.
Elmdale Rd.
P.O. Box 367
Uxbridge, MA 01569
(508) 278-2527

Classic Elite Yarns, Inc.
300-A Jackson St.
Lowell, MA 01852
(978) 453-2837

Coats & Clark, Inc.
Consumer Service Dept.
P.O. Box 12229
Greenville, SC 29612-0229
www.coatsandclark.com

JCA, Inc.
35 Scales Lane
Townsend, MA 01469
(978) 597-8794

JHB International, Inc.
1955 S. Quince St.
Denver, CO 80231
(303) 751-8100

Lion Brand Yarn
34 W. 15th St.
New York, NY 10011
(212) 243-8995

Lily Yarns
See Spinrite, Inc.

One World Button Supply Company
41 Union Square W., Room 311
New York, NY 10003
(212) 691-1331

Patons Yarns
See Spinrite, Inc.

Plymouth Yarn, Inc.
P.O. Box 28
500 Lafayette St.
Bristol, PA 19007
(215) 788-0459

Spinrite, Inc.
320 Livingstone Ave. S.
Listowel, ON
Canada N4W 3H3
(519) 291-3780

Tahki-Stacy Charles, Inc.
1059/1061 Manhattan Ave.
Brooklyn, NY 11222
(800) 962-8002

Unique Kolors, Ltd.
1428 Oak Lane
Downingtown, PA 19335
(610) 280-7720

Zecca Button Company
P.O. Box 1664
Lakeville, CT 06039
(860) 435-2211

✤ Mail Order Sources

Annie's Attic
1 Annie Lane
Big Sandy, TX 75755
(800) 582-6643

Herrschner's and Herrschner's Yarn Shoppe
2800 Hoover Rd.
Stevens Point, WI 54492
(800) 441-0838

Mary Maxim
2001 Holland Ave.
P.O. Box 5019
Port Huron, MI 48061
(800) 962-9504

Patternworks
PO Box 1690
Poughkeepsie, NY 12601
(800) 438-5464

Wool Connection
34 E. Main St.
Avon, CT 06001
(800) 933-9665

✤ Instructional

For additional technical information, refer to one of the following books.

Aytes, Barbara. *Adventures in Crocheting.* Garden City, NY: Doubleday & Co., 1972.

Blackwell, Liz. *A Treasury of Crochet Patterns.* New York: Charles Scribner's Sons, 1971.

Duncan, Ida Riley. *The Complete Book of Needlecraft.* New York: Liveright, 1972.

Goldberg, Rhoda Ochser. *The New Crochet Dictionary.* New York: Crown, 1986.

Mariano, Linda. *The Encyclopedia of Knitting and Crochet Stitch Patterns.* New York: Van Nostrand Reinhold Co., 1976.

Matthews, Anne. *Vogue Dictionary of Crochet Stitches.* London: David & Charles, 1987.

Mountford, Debra, ed., *The Harmony Guide to Crocheting Techniques and Stitches.* New York: Harmony, 1992.

Righetti, Maggie. *Crocheting in Plain English.* New York: St. Martin's Press, 1988.

Schapper, Linda P. *Complete Book of Crochet Stitch Designs.* New York: Sterling, 1985.

Threads editors. *Knitting Tips and Trade Secrets.* Newtown, CT: The Taunton Press, 1996.

Westfall, Fran. *Encyclopedia of Knitting and Crochet Stitches.* New York: Bonanza Books, 1971.

✤ Crochet Guild of America

For more information about crochet or to join the Crochet Guild of America contact:

The Crochet Guild of America
2502 Lowell Rd.
Gastonia, NC 28054
(877) 852-9190
CGOA@crochet.org
www.crochet.org